TEACHER'S PET PUBLICATIONS

PUZZLE PACK
for
Gulliver's Travels

based on the book by
Jonathan Swift

Written by
William T. Collins

© 2005 Teacher's Pet Publications
All Rights Reserved

The materials in this packet are copyrighted
by Teacher's Pet Publications, Inc.

These pages may be duplicated by the purchaser
for use in the purchaser's own classroom.

Copying any of these materials and distributing them
for any other purpose is a violation of the copyright laws.

© 2005 Teacher's Pet Publications, Inc.
www.tpet.com

INTRODUCTION
If you already own the LitPlan for this title, this Puzzle Pack will refresh your Unit Resource Materials and Vocabulary Resource Materials sections plus give you additional materials you can substitute into the tests. If you do not already have a complete LitPlan, these pages will give you some supplemental materials to use with your own plan. There are two main groups of materials: one set for unit words (such as characters' names, symbols, places, etc.) and one set for vocabulary words associated with the book.

WORD LIST
There is a word list for both the unit words and the vocabulary words. These lists show you which words are being used in the materials and the clues or definitions being used for those words. You may want to give students a word list with clues/definitions to help them, or you may want students to only have a word list (without clues/definitions) if you want them to work a little harder. Both are available for duplication. The word lists can also be your "calling key" for the bingo games.

FILL IN THE BLANK AND MATCHING
There are 4 each of the fill in the blank and matching worksheets for both the unit and vocabulary words. These pages can be used either as extra worksheets for students or as objective parts of a unit test. They can be done individually if students need extra help or as a whole class activity to review the material covered.

MAGIC SQUARES
The magic squares not only reinforce the material covered but also work on reasoning and math skills. Many teachers have told us that their students really enjoy doing these!

WORD SEARCH PUZZLES
The word search words go in all directions, as indicated on your answer keys. Two of the word search puzzles have the clues listed rather than the words. This makes the puzzle a little more difficult, but it reinforces the material better. Two word search puzzles have words only for students who find the clue puzzles too difficult.

CROSSWORD PUZZLES
Both unit and vocabulary word sections have 4 crossword puzzles.

BINGO CARDS
There are 32 individual bingo cards for the unit words and 32 individual bingo cards for the vocabulary words. You can use your word list as a "call list," calling the words at random and marking them off of your list as you go, or you could use the flash cards by cutting them apart and drawing the words at random from a hat (or box or whatever). To make a better review, you might ask for the definition and spelling of each word as you call it out—or you could call out the definitions and have students tell you the words they need to look for on the puzzle.

JUGGLE LETTERS
The vocabulary juggle letter game is intended to help students learn the spellings of the words. One sheet has the definitions listed on it as an extra help for students who need it or to reinforce the definitions if you choose to do so.

FLASH CARDS
We've included a set of vocabulary flash cards you can duplicate, cut, and fold for your students. Some teachers make a few sets for general use by the class; others make a set for each student. Some teachers duplicate them for each student and have the students cut & fold their own. You can cut out just the words and put them in a hat, have each student pick out one word and write the definition and a sentence for that word. Students then swap words and papers, with the next student adding a sentence of his own under the last one. You can have students swap as many times as you like. Each time the student will read the sentences written prior to his own and then add a sentence. You can cut out the words and definitions separately and play "I Have; Who Has?" Each student in the room draws a word and definition. The first student says, "I have (the name of the word). Who has the definition?" The student with the definition reads it then says, "I have (the name of the vocabulary word she has). Who has the definition?" The round continues until all words and definitions have been given.

Gulliver's Travels Word List

No.	Word	Clue/Definition
1.	BALNIBARBI	Continent under Laputa
2.	BIDDLE	Captain who found Gulliver near Blefuscu
3.	BLEFUSCU	Land of enemies of Lilliput
4.	BROBDINGNAG	Land of big people
5.	DUTCH	Only Europeans allowed in Japan
6.	EGGS	Proper way to break them was disputed in Lilliput
7.	ENGLAND	Gulliver's home
8.	EXTERMINATE	Houyhnhnm plan for Yahoos
9.	FARMER	Displayed Gulliver to make money
10.	FLAPPERS	Servants who hit their masters
11.	FLIMNAP	Gulliver's enemy in Lilliput
12.	FRAUD	Worst crime in Lilliput
13.	GLUBBDUBDRIB	Governor here called forth dead persons
14.	GLUMDALCLITCH	Gulliver's 'little nurse'
15.	GRAND	Houyhnhnm council meeting: ___ Assembly
16.	GULLIVER	Wrote about his adventures
17.	GUNPOWDER	King of Brobdingnag refused this gift
18.	HOPEWELL	Ship that was attacked by pirates
19.	HOUYHNHNMS	Reasoning animals
20.	IMPEACHMENT	Articles of treason against Gulliver
21.	KITE	Bird that carried Gulliver's box out to sea
22.	LAPUTA	Floating island
23.	LILLIPUT	Land of little people
24.	LINDALINO	Rebellious city in Laputa
25.	LOW	Currently in power in Lilliput: ___ Heels
26.	LUGGNAGG	Gulliver licked the king's floor here
27.	LYING	None done in land of Houyhnhnms
28.	MAIDS	Unpleasant company for Gulliver: ___ of Honor
29.	MANNIKIN	Gulliver's name in Brobdingnag
30.	MARY	Gulliver's wife
31.	MONKEY	Thought Gulliver was his young one
32.	MUNODI	Gulliver's friend in Lagado
33.	PIRATES	Set Gulliver adrift in a sloop
34.	PRIDE	Man's worst vice, according to Gulliver
35.	PROJECTORS	Academy trying new methods
36.	QUEEN	Fond of Gulliver's company in Brobdingnag
37.	SPLACKNUCK	Animal of Brobdingnag
38.	STRULDBRUGS	People who live forever
39.	SWIFT	Author of GULLIVER'S TRAVELS
40.	YAHOO	Bestial man-like creature

Gulliver's Travels Fill In The Blanks 1

1. Displayed Gulliver to make money
2. Author of GULLIVER'S TRAVELS
3. Academy trying new methods
4. Houyhnhnm plan for Yahoos
5. Thought Gulliver was his young one
6. Continent under Laputa
7. Set Gulliver adrift in a sloop
8. Fond of Gulliver's company in Brobdingnag
9. Gulliver licked the king's floor here
10. Articles of treason against Gulliver
11. Animal of Brobdingnag
12. None done in land of Houyhnhnms
13. Houyhnhnm council meeting: ___ Assembly
14. Captain who found Gulliver near Blefuscu
15. Governor here called forth dead persons
16. Man's worst vice, according to Gulliver
17. Currently in power in Lilliput: ___ Heels
18. Floating island
19. Gulliver's name in Brobdingnag
20. Land of big people

Gulliver's Travels Fill In The Blanks 1 Answer Key

FARMER	1. Displayed Gulliver to make money
SWIFT	2. Author of GULLIVER'S TRAVELS
PROJECTORS	3. Academy trying new methods
EXTERMINATE	4. Houyhnhnm plan for Yahoos
MONKEY	5. Thought Gulliver was his young one
BALNIBARBI	6. Continent under Laputa
PIRATES	7. Set Gulliver adrift in a sloop
QUEEN	8. Fond of Gulliver's company in Brobdingnag
LUGGNAGG	9. Gulliver licked the king's floor here
IMPEACHMENT	10. Articles of treason against Gulliver
SPLACKNUCK	11. Animal of Brobdingnag
LYING	12. None done in land of Houyhnhnms
GRAND	13. Houyhnhnm council meeting: ___ Assembly
BIDDLE	14. Captain who found Gulliver near Blefuscu
GLUBBDUBDRIB	15. Governor here called forth dead persons
PRIDE	16. Man's worst vice, according to Gulliver
LOW	17. Currently in power in Lilliput: ___ Heels
LAPUTA	18. Floating island
MANNIKIN	19. Gulliver's name in Brobdingnag
BROBDINGNAG	20. Land of big people

Gulliver's Travels Fill In The Blanks 2

_____ 1. Rebellious city in Laputa

_____ 2. King of Brobdingnag refused this gift

_____ 3. Land of enemies of Lilliput

_____ 4. Continent under Laputa

_____ 5. Ship that was attacked by pirates

_____ 6. Worst crime in Lilliput

_____ 7. Gulliver's wife

_____ 8. Academy trying new methods

_____ 9. Land of big people

_____ 10. Articles of treason against Gulliver

_____ 11. Animal of Brobdingnag

_____ 12. Gulliver's name in Brobdingnag

_____ 13. Man's worst vice, according to Gulliver

_____ 14. Captain who found Gulliver near Blefuscu

_____ 15. Gulliver licked the king's floor here

_____ 16. Author of GULLIVER'S TRAVELS

_____ 17. Set Gulliver adrift in a sloop

_____ 18. Gulliver's 'little nurse'

_____ 19. Displayed Gulliver to make money

_____ 20. Proper way to break them was disputed in Lilliput

Gulliver's Travels Fill In The Blanks 2 Answer Key

LINDALINO	1. Rebellious city in Laputa
GUNPOWDER	2. King of Brobdingnag refused this gift
BLEFUSCU	3. Land of enemies of Lilliput
BALNIBARBI	4. Continent under Laputa
HOPEWELL	5. Ship that was attacked by pirates
FRAUD	6. Worst crime in Lilliput
MARY	7. Gulliver's wife
PROJECTORS	8. Academy trying new methods
BROBDINGNAG	9. Land of big people
IMPEACHMENT	10. Articles of treason against Gulliver
SPLACKNUCK	11. Animal of Brobdingnag
MANNIKIN	12. Gulliver's name in Brobdingnag
PRIDE	13. Man's worst vice, according to Gulliver
BIDDLE	14. Captain who found Gulliver near Blefuscu
LUGGNAGG	15. Gulliver licked the king's floor here
SWIFT	16. Author of GULLIVER'S TRAVELS
PIRATES	17. Set Gulliver adrift in a sloop
GLUMDALCLITCH	18. Gulliver's 'little nurse'
FARMER	19. Displayed Gulliver to make money
EGGS	20. Proper way to break them was disputed in Lilliput

Gulliver's Travels Fill In The Blanks 3

_____ 1. Animal of Brobdingnag
_____ 2. Governor here called forth dead persons
_____ 3. Proper way to break them was disputed in Lilliput
_____ 4. Gulliver's name in Brobdingnag
_____ 5. Continent under Laputa
_____ 6. Unpleasant company for Gulliver: ___ of Honor
_____ 7. Displayed Gulliver to make money
_____ 8. Man's worst vice, according to Gulliver
_____ 9. Gulliver licked the king's floor here
_____ 10. King of Brobdingnag refused this gift
_____ 11. Author of GULLIVER'S TRAVELS
_____ 12. Academy trying new methods
_____ 13. Land of big people
_____ 14. Wrote about his adventures
_____ 15. Gulliver's home
_____ 16. Floating island
_____ 17. Worst crime in Lilliput
_____ 18. Bird that carried Gulliver's box out to sea
_____ 19. Set Gulliver adrift in a sloop
_____ 20. People who live forever

Gulliver's Travels Fill In The Blanks 3 Answer Key

SPLACKNUCK	1. Animal of Brobdingnag
GLUBBDUBDRIB	2. Governor here called forth dead persons
EGGS	3. Proper way to break them was disputed in Lilliput
MANNIKIN	4. Gulliver's name in Brobdingnag
BALNIBARBI	5. Continent under Laputa
MAIDS	6. Unpleasant company for Gulliver: ___ of Honor
FARMER	7. Displayed Gulliver to make money
PRIDE	8. Man's worst vice, according to Gulliver
LUGGNAGG	9. Gulliver licked the king's floor here
GUNPOWDER	10. King of Brobdingnag refused this gift
SWIFT	11. Author of GULLIVER'S TRAVELS
PROJECTORS	12. Academy trying new methods
BROBDINGNAG	13. Land of big people
GULLIVER	14. Wrote about his adventures
ENGLAND	15. Gulliver's home
LAPUTA	16. Floating island
FRAUD	17. Worst crime in Lilliput
KITE	18. Bird that carried Gulliver's box out to sea
PIRATES	19. Set Gulliver adrift in a sloop
STRULDBRUGS	20. People who live forever

Gulliver's Travels Fill In The Blanks 4

_____ 1. Land of big people

_____ 2. Houyhnhnm council meeting: ___ Assembly

_____ 3. None done in land of Houyhnhnms

_____ 4. Gulliver's 'little nurse'

_____ 5. Currently in power in Lilliput: ___ Heels

_____ 6. Gulliver licked the king's floor here

_____ 7. Gulliver's wife

_____ 8. People who live forever

_____ 9. Land of enemies of Lilliput

_____ 10. Author of GULLIVER'S TRAVELS

_____ 11. Servants who hit their masters

_____ 12. Land of little people

_____ 13. Continent under Laputa

_____ 14. Rebellious city in Laputa

_____ 15. Gulliver's friend in Lagado

_____ 16. Worst crime in Lilliput

_____ 17. Thought Gulliver was his young one

_____ 18. Proper way to break them was disputed in Lilliput

_____ 19. King of Brobdingnag refused this gift

_____ 20. Houyhnhnm plan for Yahoos

Gulliver's Travels Fill In The Blanks 4 Answer Key

BROBDINGNAG	1. Land of big people
GRAND	2. Houyhnhnm council meeting: ___ Assembly
LYING	3. None done in land of Houyhnhnms
GLUMDALCLITCH	4. Gulliver's 'little nurse'
LOW	5. Currently in power in Lilliput: ___ Heels
LUGGNAGG	6. Gulliver licked the king's floor here
MARY	7. Gulliver's wife
STRULDBRUGS	8. People who live forever
BLEFUSCU	9. Land of enemies of Lilliput
SWIFT	10. Author of GULLIVER'S TRAVELS
FLAPPERS	11. Servants who hit their masters
LILLIPUT	12. Land of little people
BALNIBARBI	13. Continent under Laputa
LINDALINO	14. Rebellious city in Laputa
MUNODI	15. Gulliver's friend in Lagado
FRAUD	16. Worst crime in Lilliput
MONKEY	17. Thought Gulliver was his young one
EGGS	18. Proper way to break them was disputed in Lilliput
GUNPOWDER	19. King of Brobdingnag refused this gift
EXTERMINATE	20. Houyhnhnm plan for Yahoos

Gulliver's Travels Matching 1

___ 1. GUNPOWDER
___ 2. DUTCH
___ 3. GULLIVER
___ 4. MONKEY
___ 5. QUEEN
___ 6. ENGLAND
___ 7. GRAND
___ 8. SPLACKNUCK
___ 9. HOUYHNHNMS
___ 10. BLEFUSCU
___ 11. MANNIKIN
___ 12. PROJECTORS
___ 13. FLIMNAP
___ 14. HOPEWELL
___ 15. BROBDINGNAG
___ 16. PRIDE
___ 17. FRAUD
___ 18. GLUBBDUBDRIB
___ 19. LAPUTA
___ 20. FLAPPERS
___ 21. FARMER
___ 22. LUGGNAGG
___ 23. PIRATES
___ 24. KITE
___ 25. MAIDS

A. Only Europeans allowed in Japan
B. Fond of Gulliver's company in Brobdingnag
C. Wrote about his adventures
D. Gulliver's enemy in Lilliput
E. Gulliver's home
F. Floating island
G. Gulliver licked the king's floor here
H. Thought Gulliver was his young one
I. Land of enemies of Lilliput
J. Academy trying new methods
K. Servants who hit their masters
L. Displayed Gulliver to make money
M. Houyhnhnm council meeting: ___ Assembly
N. Unpleasant company for Gulliver: ___ of Honor
O. Worst crime in Lilliput
P. Animal of Brobdingnag
Q. Land of big people
R. King of Brobdingnag refused this gift
S. Reasoning animals
T. Governor here called forth dead persons
U. Bird that carried Gulliver's box out to sea
V. Set Gulliver adrift in a sloop
W. Man's worst vice, according to Gulliver
X. Ship that was attacked by pirates
Y. Gulliver's name in Brobdingnag

Gulliver's Travels Matching 1 Answer Key

R - 1. GUNPOWDER	A.	Only Europeans allowed in Japan
A - 2. DUTCH	B.	Fond of Gulliver's company in Brobdingnag
C - 3. GULLIVER	C.	Wrote about his adventures
H - 4. MONKEY	D.	Gulliver's enemy in Lilliput
B - 5. QUEEN	E.	Gulliver's home
E - 6. ENGLAND	F.	Floating island
M - 7. GRAND	G.	Gulliver licked the king's floor here
P - 8. SPLACKNUCK	H.	Thought Gulliver was his young one
S - 9. HOUYHNHNMS	I.	Land of enemies of Lilliput
I - 10. BLEFUSCU	J.	Academy trying new methods
Y - 11. MANNIKIN	K.	Servants who hit their masters
J - 12. PROJECTORS	L.	Displayed Gulliver to make money
D - 13. FLIMNAP	M.	Houyhnhnm council meeting: ___ Assembly
X - 14. HOPEWELL	N.	Unpleasant company for Gulliver: ___ of Honor
Q - 15. BROBDINGNAG	O.	Worst crime in Lilliput
W - 16. PRIDE	P.	Animal of Brobdingnag
O - 17. FRAUD	Q.	Land of big people
T - 18. GLUBBDUBDRIB	R.	King of Brobdingnag refused this gift
F - 19. LAPUTA	S.	Reasoning animals
K - 20. FLAPPERS	T.	Governor here called forth dead persons
L - 21. FARMER	U.	Bird that carried Gulliver's box out to sea
G - 22. LUGGNAGG	V.	Set Gulliver adrift in a sloop
V - 23. PIRATES	W.	Man's worst vice, according to Gulliver
U - 24. KITE	X.	Ship that was attacked by pirates
N - 25. MAIDS	Y.	Gulliver's name in Brobdingnag

Gulliver's Travels Matching 2

___ 1. MUNODI A. Gulliver's 'little nurse'
___ 2. LINDALINO B. Houyhnhnm plan for Yahoos
___ 3. BIDDLE C. Worst crime in Lilliput
___ 4. GULLIVER D. Gulliver's enemy in Lilliput
___ 5. ENGLAND E. Gulliver's home
___ 6. GLUMDALCLITCH F. Bestial man-like creature
___ 7. BALNIBARBI G. Set Gulliver adrift in a sloop
___ 8. LYING H. Rebellious city in Laputa
___ 9. HOPEWELL I. Fond of Gulliver's company in Brobdingnag
___10. FARMER J. Land of big people
___11. FLIMNAP K. Wrote about his adventures
___12. MARY L. Servants who hit their masters
___13. EXTERMINATE M. Gulliver's wife
___14. LOW N. None done in land of Houyhnhnms
___15. FRAUD O. Only Europeans allowed in Japan
___16. YAHOO P. Continent under Laputa
___17. STRULDBRUGS Q. Land of enemies of Lilliput
___18. BLEFUSCU R. People who live forever
___19. BROBDINGNAG S. Gulliver licked the king's floor here
___20. FLAPPERS T. Ship that was attacked by pirates
___21. PIRATES U. Displayed Gulliver to make money
___22. DUTCH V. Governor here called forth dead persons
___23. GLUBBDUBDRIB W. Currently in power in Lilliput: ___ Heels
___24. QUEEN X. Captain who found Gulliver near Blefuscu
___25. LUGGNAGG Y. Gulliver's friend in Lagado

Gulliver's Travels Matching 2 Answer Key

Y - 1. MUNODI		A. Gulliver's 'little nurse'
H - 2. LINDALINO		B. Houyhnhnm plan for Yahoos
X - 3. BIDDLE		C. Worst crime in Lilliput
K - 4. GULLIVER		D. Gulliver's enemy in Lilliput
E - 5. ENGLAND		E. Gulliver's home
A - 6. GLUMDALCLITCH		F. Bestial man-like creature
P - 7. BALNIBARBI		G. Set Gulliver adrift in a sloop
N - 8. LYING		H. Rebellious city in Laputa
T - 9. HOPEWELL		I. Fond of Gulliver's company in Brobdingnag
U -10. FARMER		J. Land of big people
D -11. FLIMNAP		K. Wrote about his adventures
M -12. MARY		L. Servants who hit their masters
B -13. EXTERMINATE		M. Gulliver's wife
W -14. LOW		N. None done in land of Houyhnhnms
C -15. FRAUD		O. Only Europeans allowed in Japan
F -16. YAHOO		P. Continent under Laputa
R -17. STRULDBRUGS		Q. Land of enemies of Lilliput
Q -18. BLEFUSCU		R. People who live forever
J -19. BROBDINGNAG		S. Gulliver licked the king's floor here
L -20. FLAPPERS		T. Ship that was attacked by pirates
G -21. PIRATES		U. Displayed Gulliver to make money
O -22. DUTCH		V. Governor here called forth dead persons
V -23. GLUBBDUBDRIB		W. Currently in power in Lilliput: ___ Heels
I -24. QUEEN		X. Captain who found Gulliver near Blefuscu
S -25. LUGGNAGG		Y. Gulliver's friend in Lagado

Gulliver's Travels Matching 3

___ 1. MARY   A. Set Gulliver adrift in a sloop
___ 2. EXTERMINATE   B. Gulliver's wife
___ 3. BALNIBARBI   C. Man's worst vice, according to Gulliver
___ 4. LILLIPUT   D. Gulliver licked the king's floor here
___ 5. FLAPPERS   E. Wrote about his adventures
___ 6. BLEFUSCU   F. Worst crime in Lilliput
___ 7. FRAUD   G. Land of little people
___ 8. LAPUTA   H. Governor here called forth dead persons
___ 9. QUEEN   I. Currently in power in Lilliput: ___ Heels
___10. YAHOO   J. Rebellious city in Laputa
___11. PIRATES   K. Houyhnhnm council meeting: ___ Assembly
___12. LOW   L. Bestial man-like creature
___13. IMPEACHMENT   M. Reasoning animals
___14. GULLIVER   N. Articles of treason against Gulliver
___15. BROBDINGNAG   O. People who live forever
___16. GLUBBDUBDRIB   P. Displayed Gulliver to make money
___17. EGGS   Q. Floating island
___18. FARMER   R. Land of big people
___19. STRULDBRUGS   S. Proper way to break them was disputed in Lilliput
___20. LUGGNAGG   T. Academy trying new methods
___21. HOUYHNHNMS   U. Houyhnhnm plan for Yahoos
___22. GRAND   V. Land of enemies of Lilliput
___23. LINDALINO   W. Servants who hit their masters
___24. PROJECTORS   X. Continent under Laputa
___25. PRIDE   Y. Fond of Gulliver's company in Brobdingnag

Gulliver's Travels Matching 3 Answer Key

B - 1. MARY	A.	Set Gulliver adrift in a sloop
U - 2. EXTERMINATE	B.	Gulliver's wife
X - 3. BALNIBARBI	C.	Man's worst vice, according to Gulliver
G - 4. LILLIPUT	D.	Gulliver licked the king's floor here
W - 5. FLAPPERS	E.	Wrote about his adventures
V - 6. BLEFUSCU	F.	Worst crime in Lilliput
F - 7. FRAUD	G.	Land of little people
Q - 8. LAPUTA	H.	Governor here called forth dead persons
Y - 9. QUEEN	I.	Currently in power in Lilliput: ___ Heels
L - 10. YAHOO	J.	Rebellious city in Laputa
A - 11. PIRATES	K.	Houyhnhnm council meeting: ___ Assembly
I - 12. LOW	L.	Bestial man-like creature
N - 13. IMPEACHMENT	M.	Reasoning animals
E - 14. GULLIVER	N.	Articles of treason against Gulliver
R - 15. BROBDINGNAG	O.	People who live forever
H - 16. GLUBBDUBDRIB	P.	Displayed Gulliver to make money
S - 17. EGGS	Q.	Floating island
P - 18. FARMER	R.	Land of big people
O - 19. STRULDBRUGS	S.	Proper way to break them was disputed in Lilliput
D - 20. LUGGNAGG	T.	Academy trying new methods
M - 21. HOUYHNHNMS	U.	Houyhnhnm plan for Yahoos
K - 22. GRAND	V.	Land of enemies of Lilliput
J - 23. LINDALINO	W.	Servants who hit their masters
T - 24. PROJECTORS	X.	Continent under Laputa
C - 25. PRIDE	Y.	Fond of Gulliver's company in Brobdingnag

Gulliver's Travels Matching 4

___ 1. LOW
___ 2. PRIDE
___ 3. GLUMDALCLITCH
___ 4. QUEEN
___ 5. ENGLAND
___ 6. GLUBBDUBDRIB
___ 7. GULLIVER
___ 8. FLAPPERS
___ 9. STRULDBRUGS
___ 10. HOPEWELL
___ 11. EXTERMINATE
___ 12. DUTCH
___ 13. LUGGNAGG
___ 14. PIRATES
___ 15. BROBDINGNAG
___ 16. BIDDLE
___ 17. SWIFT
___ 18. LYING
___ 19. HOUYHNHNMS
___ 20. YAHOO
___ 21. FARMER
___ 22. MANNIKIN
___ 23. BALNIBARBI
___ 24. MONKEY
___ 25. GUNPOWDER

A. Displayed Gulliver to make money
B. Continent under Laputa
C. Gulliver's name in Brobdingnag
D. Bestial man-like creature
E. Houyhnhnm plan for Yahoos
F. Currently in power in Lilliput: ___ Heels
G. Gulliver's home
H. Ship that was attacked by pirates
I. Fond of Gulliver's company in Brobdingnag
J. Captain who found Gulliver near Blefuscu
K. King of Brobdingnag refused this gift
L. Set Gulliver adrift in a sloop
M. Only Europeans allowed in Japan
N. People who live forever
O. Man's worst vice, according to Gulliver
P. Gulliver's 'little nurse'
Q. Author of GULLIVER'S TRAVELS
R. Reasoning animals
S. Gulliver licked the king's floor here
T. Governor here called forth dead persons
U. Servants who hit their masters
V. Thought Gulliver was his young one
W. Wrote about his adventures
X. None done in land of Houyhnhnms
Y. Land of big people

Gulliver's Travels Matching 4 Answer Key

F - 1. LOW	A.	Displayed Gulliver to make money
O - 2. PRIDE	B.	Continent under Laputa
P - 3. GLUMDALCLITCH	C.	Gulliver's name in Brobdingnag
I - 4. QUEEN	D.	Bestial man-like creature
G - 5. ENGLAND	E.	Houyhnhnm plan for Yahoos
T - 6. GLUBBDUBDRIB	F.	Currently in power in Lilliput: ___ Heels
W - 7. GULLIVER	G.	Gulliver's home
U - 8. FLAPPERS	H.	Ship that was attacked by pirates
N - 9. STRULDBRUGS	I.	Fond of Gulliver's company in Brobdingnag
H -10. HOPEWELL	J.	Captain who found Gulliver near Blefuscu
E -11. EXTERMINATE	K.	King of Brobdingnag refused this gift
M -12. DUTCH	L.	Set Gulliver adrift in a sloop
S -13. LUGGNAGG	M.	Only Europeans allowed in Japan
L -14. PIRATES	N.	People who live forever
Y -15. BROBDINGNAG	O.	Man's worst vice, according to Gulliver
J -16. BIDDLE	P.	Gulliver's 'little nurse'
Q -17. SWIFT	Q.	Author of GULLIVER'S TRAVELS
X -18. LYING	R.	Reasoning animals
R -19. HOUYHNHNMS	S.	Gulliver licked the king's floor here
D -20. YAHOO	T.	Governor here called forth dead persons
A -21. FARMER	U.	Servants who hit their masters
C -22. MANNIKIN	V.	Thought Gulliver was his young one
B -23. BALNIBARBI	W.	Wrote about his adventures
V -24. MONKEY	X.	None done in land of Houyhnhnms
K -25. GUNPOWDER	Y.	Land of big people

Gulliver's Travels Magic Squares 1

A. GLUBBDUBDRIB
B. MONKEY
C. SPLACKNUCK
D. FLIMNAP
E. LOW
F. GLUMDALCLITCH
G. STRULDBRUGS
H. GRAND
I. KITE
J. PROJECTORS
K. BIDDLE
L. EXTERMINATE
M. HOUYHNHNMS
N. FRAUD
O. MUNODI
P. FARMER

1. Animal of Brobdingnag
2. Academy trying new methods
3. Gulliver's 'little nurse'
4. Gulliver's friend in Lagado
5. Displayed Gulliver to make money
6. Currently in power in Lilliput: ___ Heels
7. Bird that carried Gulliver's box out to sea
8. Gulliver's enemy in Lilliput
9. Reasoning animals
10. Houyhnhnm council meeting: ___ Assembly
11. Houyhnhnm plan for Yahoos
12. Governor here called forth dead persons
13. Thought Gulliver was his young one
14. Captain who found Gulliver near Blefuscu
15. People who live forever
16. Worst crime in Lilliput

A=	B=	C=	D=
E=	F=	G=	H=
I=	J=	K=	L=
M=	N=	O=	P=

Gulliver's Travels Magic Squares 1 Answer Key

A. GLUBBDUBDRIB
B. MONKEY
C. SPLACKNUCK
D. FLIMNAP
E. LOW
F. GLUMDALCLITCH
G. STRULDBRUGS
H. GRAND
I. KITE
J. PROJECTORS
K. BIDDLE
L. EXTERMINATE
M. HOUYHNHNMS
N. FRAUD
O. MUNODI
P. FARMER

1. Animal of Brobdingnag
2. Academy trying new methods
3. Gulliver's 'little nurse'
4. Gulliver's friend in Lagado
5. Displayed Gulliver to make money
6. Currently in power in Lilliput: ___ Heels
7. Bird that carried Gulliver's box out to sea
8. Gulliver's enemy in Lilliput
9. Reasoning animals
10. Houyhnhnm council meeting: ___ Assembly
11. Houyhnhnm plan for Yahoos
12. Governor here called forth dead persons
13. Thought Gulliver was his young one
14. Captain who found Gulliver near Blefuscu
15. People who live forever
16. Worst crime in Lilliput

A=12	B=13	C=1	D=8
E=6	F=3	G=15	H=10
I=7	J=2	K=14	L=11
M=9	N=16	O=4	P=5

Gulliver's Travels Magic Squares 2

A. BLEFUSCU
B. GUNPOWDER
C. GULLIVER
D. MUNODI
E. GLUBBDUBDRIB
F. FARMER
G. MAIDS
H. DUTCH
I. ENGLAND
J. GLUMDALCLITCH
K. MONKEY
L. YAHOO
M. EXTERMINATE
N. BROBDINGNAG
O. LILLIPUT
P. LAPUTA

1. King of Brobdingnag refused this gift
2. Unpleasant company for Gulliver: ___ of Honor
3. Thought Gulliver was his young one
4. Land of big people
5. Houyhnhnm plan for Yahoos
6. Bestial man-like creature
7. Only Europeans allowed in Japan
8. Land of enemies of Lilliput
9. Floating island
10. Gulliver's home
11. Governor here called forth dead persons
12. Gulliver's friend in Lagado
13. Wrote about his adventures
14. Displayed Gulliver to make money
15. Gulliver's 'little nurse'
16. Land of little people

A=	B=	C=	D=
E=	F=	G=	H=
I=	J=	K=	L=
M=	N=	O=	P=

Gulliver's Travels Magic Squares 2 Answer Key

A. BLEFUSCU
B. GUNPOWDER
C. GULLIVER
D. MUNODI
E. GLUBBDUBDRIB
F. FARMER
G. MAIDS
H. DUTCH
I. ENGLAND
J. GLUMDALCLITCH
K. MONKEY
L. YAHOO
M. EXTERMINATE
N. BROBDINGNAG
O. LILLIPUT
P. LAPUTA

1. King of Brobdingnag refused this gift
2. Unpleasant company for Gulliver: ___ of Honor
3. Thought Gulliver was his young one
4. Land of big people
5. Houyhnhnm plan for Yahoos
6. Bestial man-like creature
7. Only Europeans allowed in Japan
8. Land of enemies of Lilliput
9. Floating island
10. Gulliver's home
11. Governor here called forth dead persons
12. Gulliver's friend in Lagado
13. Wrote about his adventures
14. Displayed Gulliver to make money
15. Gulliver's 'little nurse'
16. Land of little people

A=8	B=1	C=13	D=12
E=11	F=14	G=2	H=7
I=10	J=15	K=3	L=6
M=5	N=4	O=16	P=9

Gulliver's Travels Magic Squares 3

A. GULLIVER
B. LINDALINO
C. LYING
D. GLUMDALCLITCH
E. MUNODI
F. PRIDE
G. FRAUD
H. STRULDBRUGS
I. MAIDS
J. DUTCH
K. LOW
L. QUEEN
M. YAHOO
N. IMPEACHMENT
O. GRAND
P. BALNIBARBI

1. None done in land of Houyhnhnms
2. Only Europeans allowed in Japan
3. Man's worst vice, according to Gulliver
4. Houyhnhnm council meeting: ___ Assembly
5. Continent under Laputa
6. Gulliver's friend in Lagado
7. Unpleasant company for Gulliver: ___ of Honor
8. Gulliver's 'little nurse'
9. Bestial man-like creature
10. People who live forever
11. Fond of Gulliver's company in Brobdingnag
12. Wrote about his adventures
13. Rebellious city in Laputa
14. Currently in power in Lilliput: ___ Heels
15. Worst crime in Lilliput
16. Articles of treason against Gulliver

A=	B=	C=	D=
E=	F=	G=	H=
I=	J=	K=	L=
M=	N=	O=	P=

Gulliver's Travels Magic Squares 3 Answer Key

A. GULLIVER
B. LINDALINO
C. LYING
D. GLUMDALCLITCH
E. MUNODI
F. PRIDE
G. FRAUD
H. STRULDBRUGS
I. MAIDS
J. DUTCH
K. LOW
L. QUEEN
M. YAHOO
N. IMPEACHMENT
O. GRAND
P. BALNIBARBI

1. None done in land of Houyhnhnms
2. Only Europeans allowed in Japan
3. Man's worst vice, according to Gulliver
4. Houyhnhnm council meeting: ___ Assembly
5. Continent under Laputa
6. Gulliver's friend in Lagado
7. Unpleasant company for Gulliver: ___ of Honor
8. Gulliver's 'little nurse'
9. Bestial man-like creature
10. People who live forever
11. Fond of Gulliver's company in Brobdingnag
12. Wrote about his adventures
13. Rebellious city in Laputa
14. Currently in power in Lilliput: ___ Heels
15. Worst crime in Lilliput
16. Articles of treason against Gulliver

A=12	B=13	C=1	D=8
E=6	F=3	G=15	H=10
I=7	J=2	K=14	L=11
M=9	N=16	O=4	P=5

Gulliver's Travels Magic Squares 4

A. MUNODI
B. ENGLAND
C. PRIDE
D. GRAND
E. MARY
F. GLUBBDUBDRIB
G. BIDDLE
H. BALNIBARBI
I. GLUMDALCLITCH
J. EXTERMINATE
K. HOPEWELL
L. BROBDINGNAG
M. STRULDBRUGS
N. QUEEN
O. MANNIKIN
P. SWIFT

1. Continent under Laputa
2. Gulliver's friend in Lagado
3. Gulliver's home
4. Captain who found Gulliver near Blefuscu
5. Houyhnhnm plan for Yahoos
6. Gulliver's name in Brobdingnag
7. Author of GULLIVER'S TRAVELS
8. Gulliver's 'little nurse'
9. Ship that was attacked by pirates
10. Fond of Gulliver's company in Brobdingnag
11. People who live forever
12. Land of big people
13. Gulliver's wife
14. Houyhnhnm council meeting: ___ Assembly
15. Man's worst vice, according to Gulliver
16. Governor here called forth dead persons

A=	B=	C=	D=
E=	F=	G=	H=
I=	J=	K=	L=
M=	N=	O=	P=

Gulliver's Travels Magic Squares 4 Answer Key

A. MUNODI
B. ENGLAND
C. PRIDE
D. GRAND
E. MARY
F. GLUBBDUBDRIB
G. BIDDLE
H. BALNIBARBI
I. GLUMDALCLITCH
J. EXTERMINATE
K. HOPEWELL
L. BROBDINGNAG
M. STRULDBRUGS
N. QUEEN
O. MANNIKIN
P. SWIFT

1. Continent under Laputa
2. Gulliver's friend in Lagado
3. Gulliver's home
4. Captain who found Gulliver near Blefuscu
5. Houyhnhnm plan for Yahoos
6. Gulliver's name in Brobdingnag
7. Author of GULLIVER'S TRAVELS
8. Gulliver's 'little nurse'
9. Ship that was attacked by pirates
10. Fond of Gulliver's company in Brobdingnag
11. People who live forever
12. Land of big people
13. Gulliver's wife
14. Houyhnhnm council meeting: ___ Assembly
15. Man's worst vice, according to Gulliver
16. Governor here called forth dead persons

A=2	B=3	C=15	D=14
E=13	F=16	G=4	H=1
I=8	J=5	K=9	L=12
M=11	N=10	O=6	P=7

Gulliver's Travels Word Search 1

```
G P M G B S G L U B B D U B D R I B I Y
U L I B R A J J I N D M D G C X S S M X
N L U R X A L B R N H R D Y W P T P P C
P F T M A W N N P P D T Q L E R L E G
O W K N D T Y D I Q R A D I X Q U A A K
W D P L S A E F N B N X L T S R L C C B
D M R W V J L S H V A L E I M H D K H Z
E C O G M V R C B F I R K T N V B N M B
R C J N P D Q F L P M T B L H O R U E J
B N E Y K D F F U I T W K I N W U C N F
C C C N T E F T N H T L S W H D G K T V
N D T B G X Y A M B W C B D Y F S Y D H
G L O Z V L T J U H B R H C U H T N X Q
U K R D Q E A Z N H O T E P O Q F V Q F
L J S W R R Z N O B X H G K H W Z F D F
L A L G H C T U D L U G G N A G G T Y F
I L P G M B L I I S E R S S N F F D J P
V J K U O H N K V D B P J I K S L T T J
E J V O T G M T I Y S X Y W R G A F X D
R K H K N A F R A U D L L E W E P O H C
W A T A I I P Q P Y C O M X Q T P F G P
Y H G D W T S M U D W R D L M Q E P D N
X B S S F W E A X E A Q M X N P R S Z T
F L I M N A P R J F E B L E F U S C U P
B I D D L E W Y M A N N I K I N D P J Y
```

Academy trying new methods (10)
Animal of Brobdingnag (10)
Articles of treason against Gulliver (11)
Author of GULLIVER'S TRAVELS (5)
Bestial man-like creature (5)
Bird that carried Gulliver's box out to sea (4)
Captain who found Gulliver near Blefuscu (6)
Continent under Laputa (10)
Currently in power in Lilliput: ___ Heels (3)
Displayed Gulliver to make money (6)
Floating island (6)
Fond of Gulliver's company in Brobdingnag (5)
Governor here called forth dead persons (12)
Gulliver licked the king's floor here (8)
Gulliver's 'little nurse' (13)
Gulliver's enemy in Lilliput (7)
Gulliver's friend in Lagado (6)
Gulliver's home (7)
Gulliver's name in Brobdingnag (8)
Gulliver's wife (4)
Houyhnhnm council meeting: ___ Assembly (5)

Houyhnhnm plan for Yahoos (11)
King of Brobdingnag refused this gift (9)
Land of big people (11)
Land of enemies of Lilliput (8)
Land of little people (8)
Man's worst vice, according to Gulliver (5)
None done in land of Houyhnhnms (5)
Only Europeans allowed in Japan (5)
People who live forever (11)
Proper way to break them was disputed in Lilliput (4)
Reasoning animals (10)
Rebellious city in Laputa (9)
Servants who hit their masters (8)
Set Gulliver adrift in a sloop (7)
Ship that was attacked by pirates (8)
Thought Gulliver was his young one (6)
Unpleasant company for Gulliver: ___ of Honor (5)
Worst crime in Lilliput (5)
Wrote about his adventures (8)

Gulliver's Travels Word Search 1 Answer Key

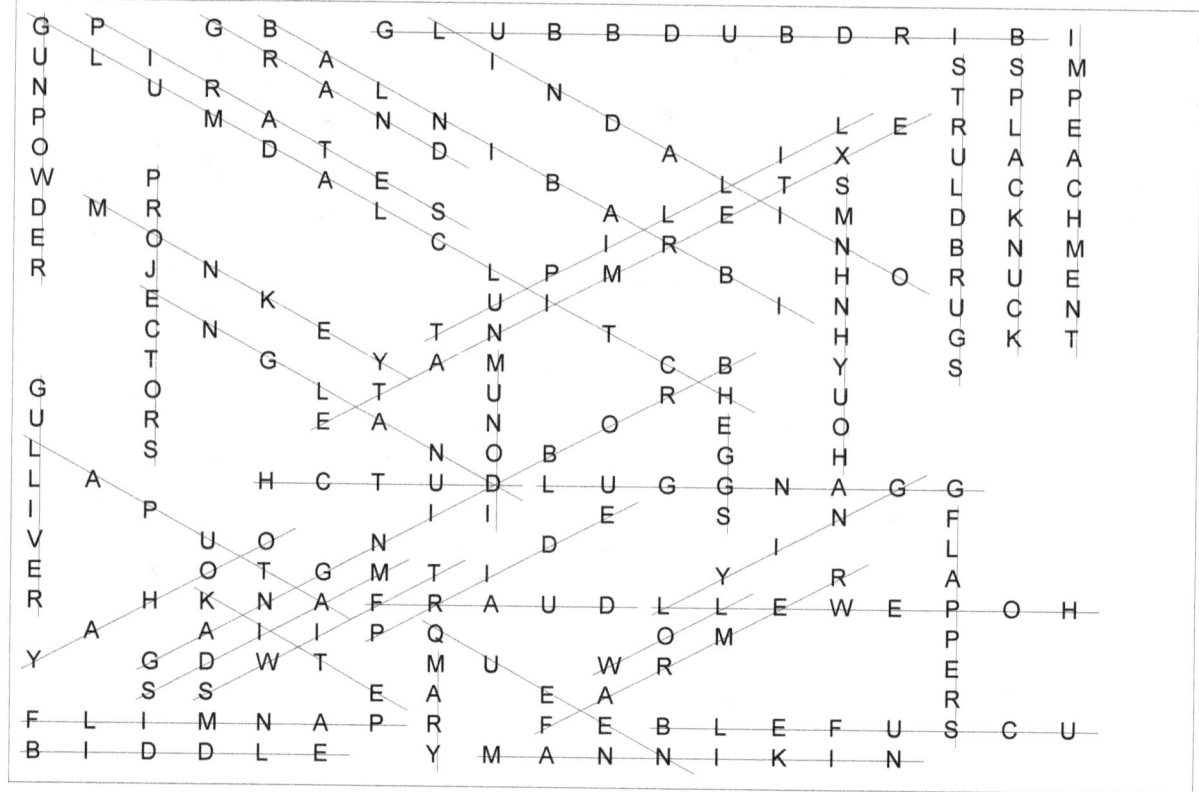

Academy trying new methods (10)
Animal of Brobdingnag (10)
Articles of treason against Gulliver (11)
Author of GULLIVER'S TRAVELS (5)
Bestial man-like creature (5)
Bird that carried Gulliver's box out to sea (4)
Captain who found Gulliver near Blefuscu (6)
Continent under Laputa (10)
Currently in power in Lilliput: ___ Heels (3)
Displayed Gulliver to make money (6)
Floating island (6)
Fond of Gulliver's company in Brobdingnag (5)
Governor here called forth dead persons (12)
Gulliver licked the king's floor here (8)
Gulliver's 'little nurse' (13)
Gulliver's enemy in Lilliput (7)
Gulliver's friend in Lagado (6)
Gulliver's home (7)
Gulliver's name in Brobdingnag (8)
Gulliver's wife (4)
Houyhnhnm council meeting: ___ Assembly (5)

Houyhnhnm plan for Yahoos (11)
King of Brobdingnag refused this gift (9)
Land of big people (11)
Land of enemies of Lilliput (8)
Land of little people (8)
Man's worst vice, according to Gulliver (5)
None done in land of Houyhnhnms (5)
Only Europeans allowed in Japan (5)
People who live forever (11)
Proper way to break them was disputed in Lilliput (4)
Reasoning animals (10)
Rebellious city in Laputa (9)
Servants who hit their masters (8)
Set Gulliver adrift in a sloop (7)
Ship that was attacked by pirates (8)
Thought Gulliver was his young one (6)
Unpleasant company for Gulliver: ___ of Honor (5)
Worst crime in Lilliput (5)
Wrote about his adventures (8)

Gulliver's Travels Word Search 2

```
I M P E A C H M E N T P N H G F B S W M
S C Z Q Q C T F V P R I S O L L L T K D
P P H M F U N R T O K Y D U U A E R J V
L F I X C R E U J I J Y S Y B P F U W R
A M K R V F P E N H M J E H B P U L M L
C K Z L A I C N N V X X O N D E S D B S
K S P J L T A R D C T P Y H U R C B H C
N B M L O M E T L E E Z M N B S U R M D
U C I R G K Q S R W H N Q M D G Z U U P
C L S Y R F K M E L T M W S R U Q G N P
K E F Q D R I L H H T P M R I N B S O L
G N Z L R N L G G K P Z T W B P V Z D X
L G Y F A J X H C D B Y E K N O M Q I W
U L F T V P C G H G S G F L O W M D B Z
M A E R D K U S G Z G Z G H T D Z J M X
D N I T A M D T R G Y H A F M E D Z J D
A D B B Y U V T A L S Y I Z F R R D W T
L N R R Q S D N N I Y W F T G E L O C B
C T A F J H G R D N S I J W M V L F Z E
L M B F V G B C D D Q Z N R V I E L T H
I H I D U Z S D I A M R A G E L W I J X
T K N L U G M H K L J F M S D L K M R F
C T L Z G T R N C I T T B D I U W N J F
H V A E S K C T D N L K I K R G K A B F
B W B W Z F Y H M O N B W H P C G P R S
```

Academy trying new methods (10)
Animal of Brobdingnag (10)
Articles of treason against Gulliver (11)
Author of GULLIVER'S TRAVELS (5)
Bestial man-like creature (5)
Bird that carried Gulliver's box out to sea (4)
Captain who found Gulliver near Blefuscu (6)
Continent under Laputa (10)
Currently in power in Lilliput: ___ Heels (3)
Displayed Gulliver to make money (6)
Floating island (6)
Fond of Gulliver's company in Brobdingnag (5)
Governor here called forth dead persons (12)
Gulliver licked the king's floor here (8)
Gulliver's 'little nurse' (13)
Gulliver's enemy in Lilliput (7)
Gulliver's friend in Lagado (6)
Gulliver's home (7)
Gulliver's name in Brobdingnag (8)
Gulliver's wife (4)
Houyhnhnm council meeting: ___ Assembly (5)

Houyhnhnm plan for Yahoos (11)
King of Brobdingnag refused this gift (9)
Land of enemies of Lilliput (8)
Land of little people (8)
Man's worst vice, according to Gulliver (5)
None done in land of Houyhnhnms (5)
Only Europeans allowed in Japan (5)
People who live forever (11)
Proper way to break them was disputed in Lilliput (4)
Reasoning animals (10)
Rebellious city in Laputa (9)
Servants who hit their masters (8)
Set Gulliver adrift in a sloop (7)
Ship that was attacked by pirates (8)
Thought Gulliver was his young one (6)
Unpleasant company for Gulliver: ___ of Honor (5)
Worst crime in Lilliput (5)
Wrote about his adventures (8)

Gulliver's Travels Word Search 2 Answer Key

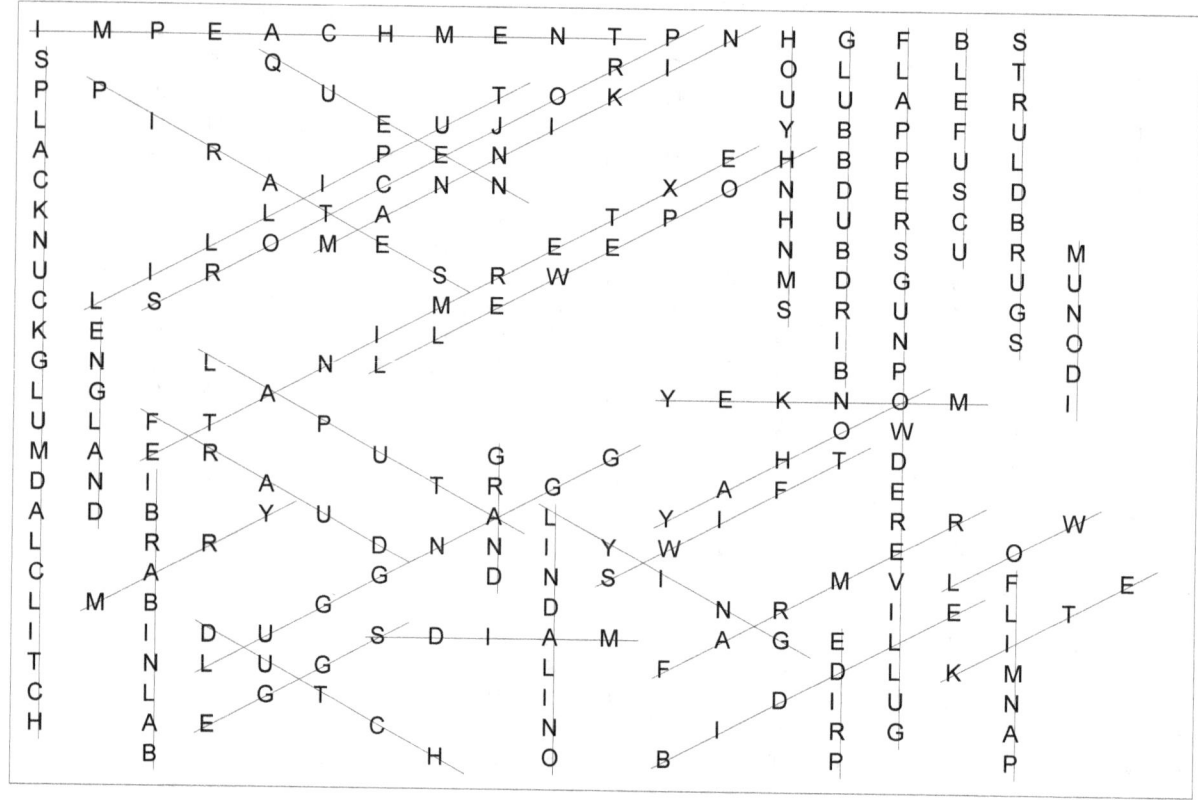

Academy trying new methods (10)
Animal of Brobdingnag (10)
Articles of treason against Gulliver (11)
Author of GULLIVER'S TRAVELS (5)
Bestial man-like creature (5)
Bird that carried Gulliver's box out to sea (4)
Captain who found Gulliver near Blefuscu (6)
Continent under Laputa (10)
Currently in power in Lilliput: ___ Heels (3)
Displayed Gulliver to make money (6)
Floating island (6)
Fond of Gulliver's company in Brobdingnag (5)
Governor here called forth dead persons (12)
Gulliver licked the king's floor here (8)
Gulliver's 'little nurse' (13)
Gulliver's enemy in Lilliput (7)
Gulliver's friend in Lagado (6)
Gulliver's home (7)
Gulliver's name in Brobdingnag (8)
Gulliver's wife (4)
Houyhnhnm council meeting: ___ Assembly (5)
Houyhnhnm plan for Yahoos (11)
King of Brobdingnag refused this gift (9)
Land of enemies of Lilliput (8)
Land of little people (8)
Man's worst vice, according to Gulliver (5)
None done in land of Houyhnhnms (5)
Only Europeans allowed in Japan (5)
People who live forever (11)
Proper way to break them was disputed in Lilliput (4)
Reasoning animals (10)
Rebellious city in Laputa (9)
Servants who hit their masters (8)
Set Gulliver adrift in a sloop (7)
Ship that was attacked by pirates (8)
Thought Gulliver was his young one (6)
Unpleasant company for Gulliver: ___ of Honor (5)
Worst crime in Lilliput (5)
Wrote about his adventures (8)

Gulliver's Travels Word Search 3

```
L S T R U L D B R U G S M B V B G S B J
I B I R D U D B B U L G A G J L P L M
L S M M K J H Y P J D W T L G M U L E N
L N C G P B R O B D I N G N A G M A F L
I K E X T E R A M I N A T E I N P D C U L
P H B X G H A P Y J P H X B G T A K S V
U Z C K O Q M C Q L R D Y A G B L N C J
T D H D N V X F H X O W L R U V C U X F
G Z O Y I W N F Z M J L N B L Q L C X Z
G B P S L Z L H Q E K Y I C D I K F T
K R E W A R C I H L C N X P P V T H F D
X M W P D O Q M V N T V T R M K C C L C
J A E B N O Z N G L O F J I L A H T H B
X R L D I H K A A H R Q F D R K I U W L
S Y L F L A P P E R S G G E B I D D L E
F X B Y R Y U G X M M W D W H R A N N S G
Y B I L N T B B N L D W I X H A Q A U B
F N H O A K M H P T O T K F R P N L L P
G R S W L C N A T P P R I G T E I R G Y G
F T A J H H P X N Y L C T D E V P W N N I
C A Z U Y B W U E N Y W E U P W E D J
G K R U D P G K Y Z I G Q E P Y D O S P
Q P O M H Q N K T Z H K R B N T N N R C
Q H X R E O F S E T A R I P Y U M H L K
F R R V M R H J Q X K H F N M X R F F P
```

BALNIBARBI	FLIMNAP	KITE	MONKEY
BIDDLE	FRAUD	LAPUTA	MUNODI
BLEFUSCU	GLUBBDUBDRIB	LILLIPUT	PIRATES
BROBDINGNAG	GLUMDALCLITCH	LINDALINO	PRIDE
DUTCH	GRAND	LOW	PROJECTORS
EGGS	GULLIVER	LUGGNAGG	QUEEN
ENGLAND	GUNPOWDER	LYING	SPLACKNUCK
EXTERMINATE	HOPEWELL	MAIDS	STRULDBRUGS
FARMER	HOUYHNHNMS	MANNIKIN	SWIFT
FLAPPERS	IMPEACHMENT	MARY	YAHOO

Gulliver's Travels Word Search 3 Answer Key

BALNIBARBI	FLIMNAP	KITE	MONKEY
BIDDLE	FRAUD	LAPUTA	MUNODI
BLEFUSCU	GLUBBDUBDRIB	LILLIPUT	PIRATES
BROBDINGNAG	GLUMDALCLITCH	LINDALINO	PRIDE
DUTCH	GRAND	LOW	PROJECTORS
EGGS	GULLIVER	LUGGNAGG	QUEEN
ENGLAND	GUNPOWDER	LYING	SPLACKNUCK
EXTERMINATE	HOPEWELL	MAIDS	STRULDBRUGS
FARMER	HOUYHNHNMS	MANNIKIN	SWIFT
FLAPPERS	IMPEACHMENT	MARY	YAHOO

Gulliver's Travels Word Search 4

```
G L U M D A L C L I T C H B L J Z M M Z
L S T R U L D B R J U G S H B I U X Z S V
E X Z J X Q W D J N S H H R G P Z L N P
F X T N E M H C A E P M I D G X L I C
H D T G J F X O Q L T T B N M N D Z
C T B E L X J S P Y C K C U A X S K A D
G L L C R K C H C E D Q Q D G S Z I L T
K C L B X M N Z P R W R X B G C D N B K
G P M P Y I F I F D E P B F J N I P
M Y R D Q M N R N Y J L U A A R G O S
D U T C H K S E A T U P A M O E G M N S
C P G Z E L D T T P I G V W L V E L
J G A K V W G D E S E M T C I P R I D P
F N N X O N B D S W N S G O P R J T U R
S O G P E H A I N A D N L O W Y J U J
M Z N L Q O L B P I I L M O D Y I Z Q K
Y U I I B U N P A Y U G B H F K N L D D
G D D L Z Y I M L G S P L A C K K N C K
D D B L N H B N B L E E F Y X G A R N
M S O I X N N O D S W E G F B X R H W Y Q
D H R P Q H A R O N P S U W F S X K Z F
N T B U W N B B I D R L T A J C B M I F T G V Z
G Q M T J M I T L B L W S L F Y J S H C Y
K W S M N S X O R S F D Z B L T F N R D
P R O J E C T O R S
```

BALNIBARBI   FLIMNAP   KITE   MONKEY

BIDDLE   FRAUD   LAPUTA   MUNODI

BLEFUSCU   GLUBBDUBDRIB   LILLIPUT   PIRATES

BROBDINGNAG   GLUMDALCLITCH   LINDALINO   PRIDE

DUTCH   GRAND   LOW   PROJECTORS

EGGS   GULLIVER   LUGGNAGG   QUEEN

ENGLAND   GUNPOWDER   LYING   SPLACKNUCK

EXTERMINATE   HOPEWELL   MAIDS   STRULDBRUGS

FARMER   HOUYHNHNMS   MANNIKIN   SWIFT

FLAPPERS   IMPEACHMENT   MARY   YAHOO

Gulliver's Travels Word Search 4 Answer Key

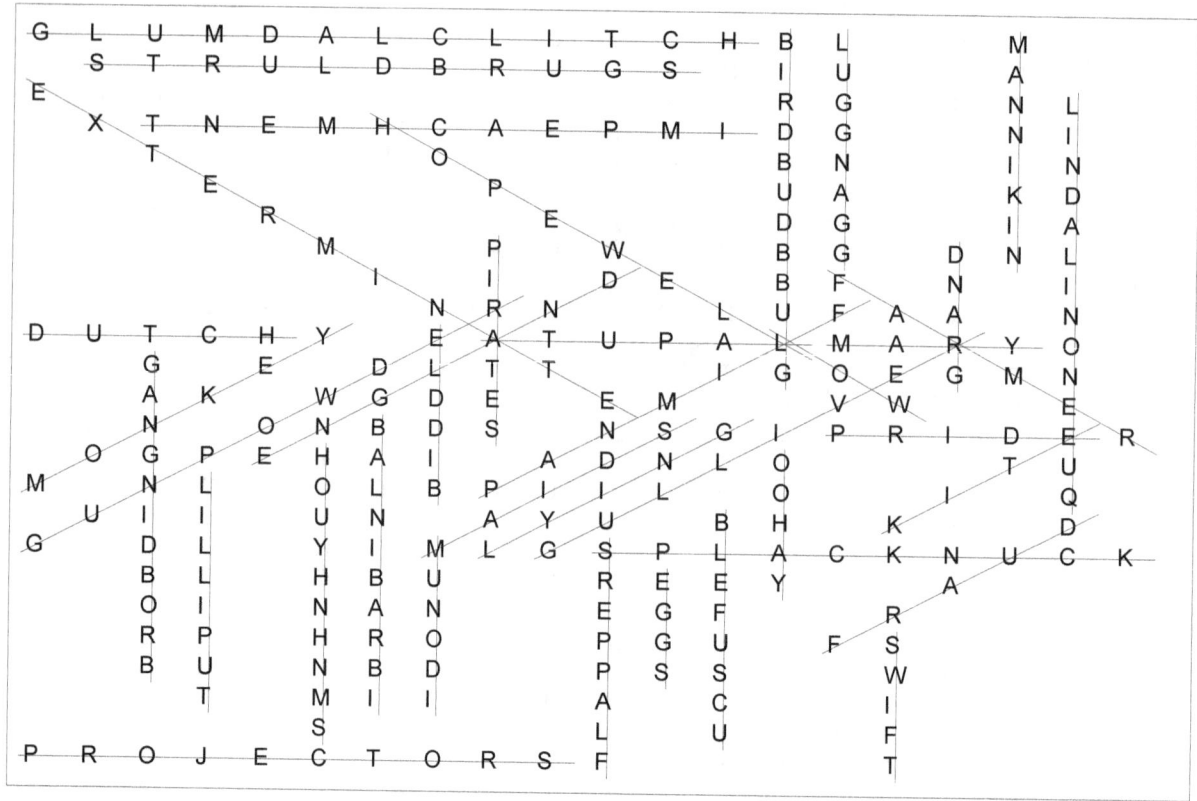

BALNIBARBI	FLIMNAP	KITE	MONKEY
BIDDLE	FRAUD	LAPUTA	MUNODI
BLEFUSCU	GLUBBDUBDRIB	LILLIPUT	PIRATES
BROBDINGNAG	GLUMDALCLITCH	LINDALINO	PRIDE
DUTCH	GRAND	LOW	PROJECTORS
EGGS	GULLIVER	LUGGNAGG	QUEEN
ENGLAND	GUNPOWDER	LYING	SPLACKNUCK
EXTERMINATE	HOPEWELL	MAIDS	STRULDBRUGS
FARMER	HOUYHNHNMS	MANNIKIN	SWIFT
FLAPPERS	IMPEACHMENT	MARY	YAHOO

Gulliver's Travels Crossword 1

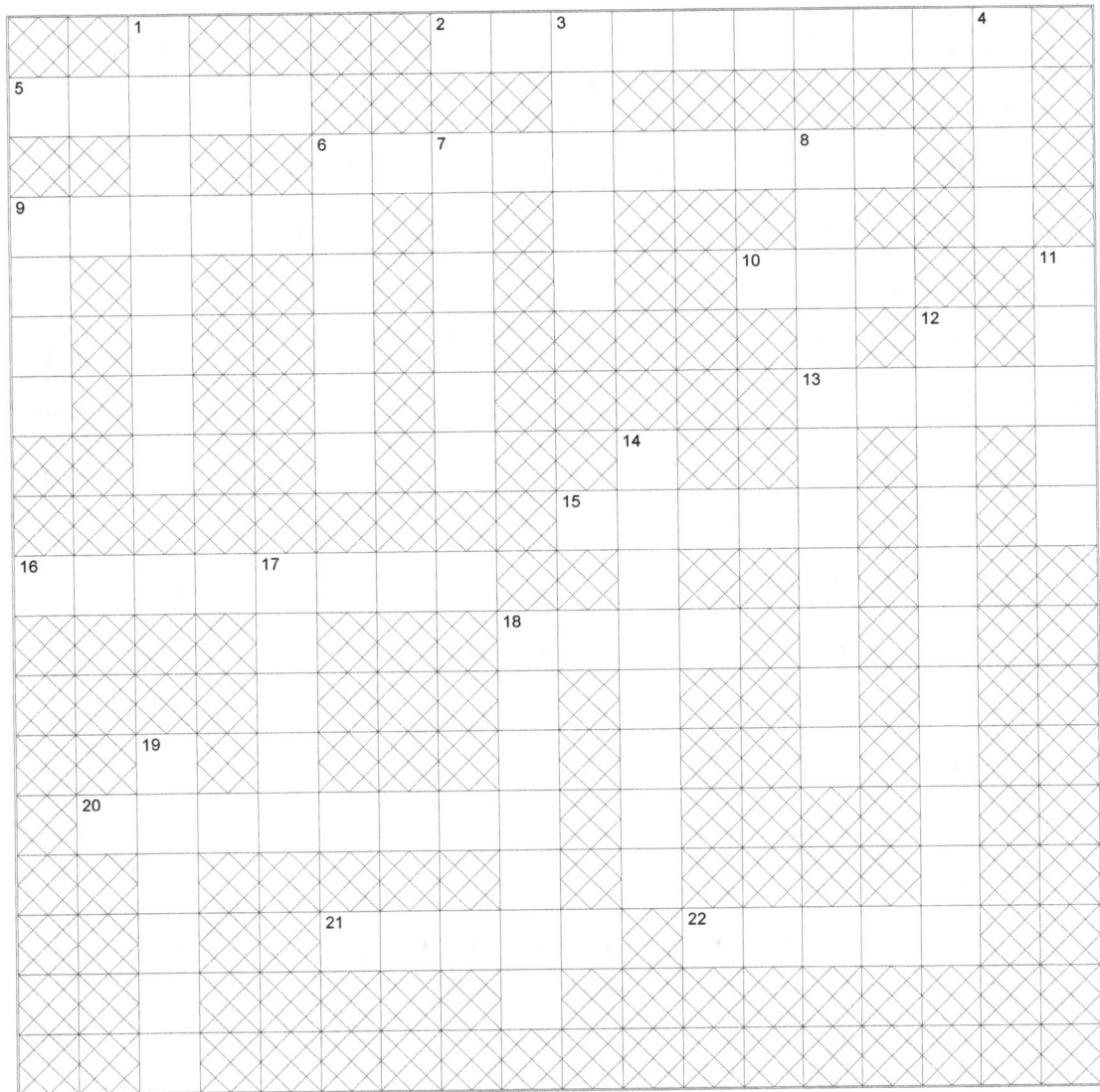

Across
2. Animal of Brobdingnag
5. Worst crime in Lilliput
6. Continent under Laputa
9. Gulliver's friend in Lagado
10. Currently in power in Lilliput: ___ Heels
13. Only Europeans allowed in Japan
15. Fond of Gulliver's company in Brobdingnag
16. Servants who hit their masters
18. Proper way to break them was disputed in Lilliput
20. Ship that was attacked by pirates
21. Houyhnhnm council meeting: ___ Assembly
22. Unpleasant company for Gulliver: ___ of Honor

Down
1. Gulliver's name in Brobdingnag
3. None done in land of Houyhnhnms
4. Bird that carried Gulliver's box out to sea
6. Captain who found Gulliver near Blefuscu
7. Floating island
8. Land of big people
9. Gulliver's wife
11. Bestial man-like creature
12. People who live forever
14. Gulliver licked the king's floor here
17. Man's worst vice, according to Gulliver
18. Gulliver's home
19. Thought Gulliver was his young one

Gulliver's Travels Crossword 1 Answer Key

Across
2. Animal of Brobdingnag
5. Worst crime in Lilliput
6. Continent under Laputa
9. Gulliver's friend in Lagado
10. Currently in power in Lilliput: ___ Heels
13. Only Europeans allowed in Japan
15. Fond of Gulliver's company in Brobdingnag
16. Servants who hit their masters
18. Proper way to break them was disputed in Lilliput
20. Ship that was attacked by pirates
21. Houyhnhnm council meeting: ___ Assembly
22. Unpleasant company for Gulliver: ___ of Honor

Down
1. Gulliver's name in Brobdingnag
3. None done in land of Houyhnhnms
4. Bird that carried Gulliver's box out to sea
6. Captain who found Gulliver near Blefuscu
7. Floating island
8. Land of big people
9. Gulliver's wife
11. Bestial man-like creature
12. People who live forever
14. Gulliver licked the king's floor here
17. Man's worst vice, according to Gulliver
18. Gulliver's home
19. Thought Gulliver was his young one

Gulliver's Travels Crossword 2

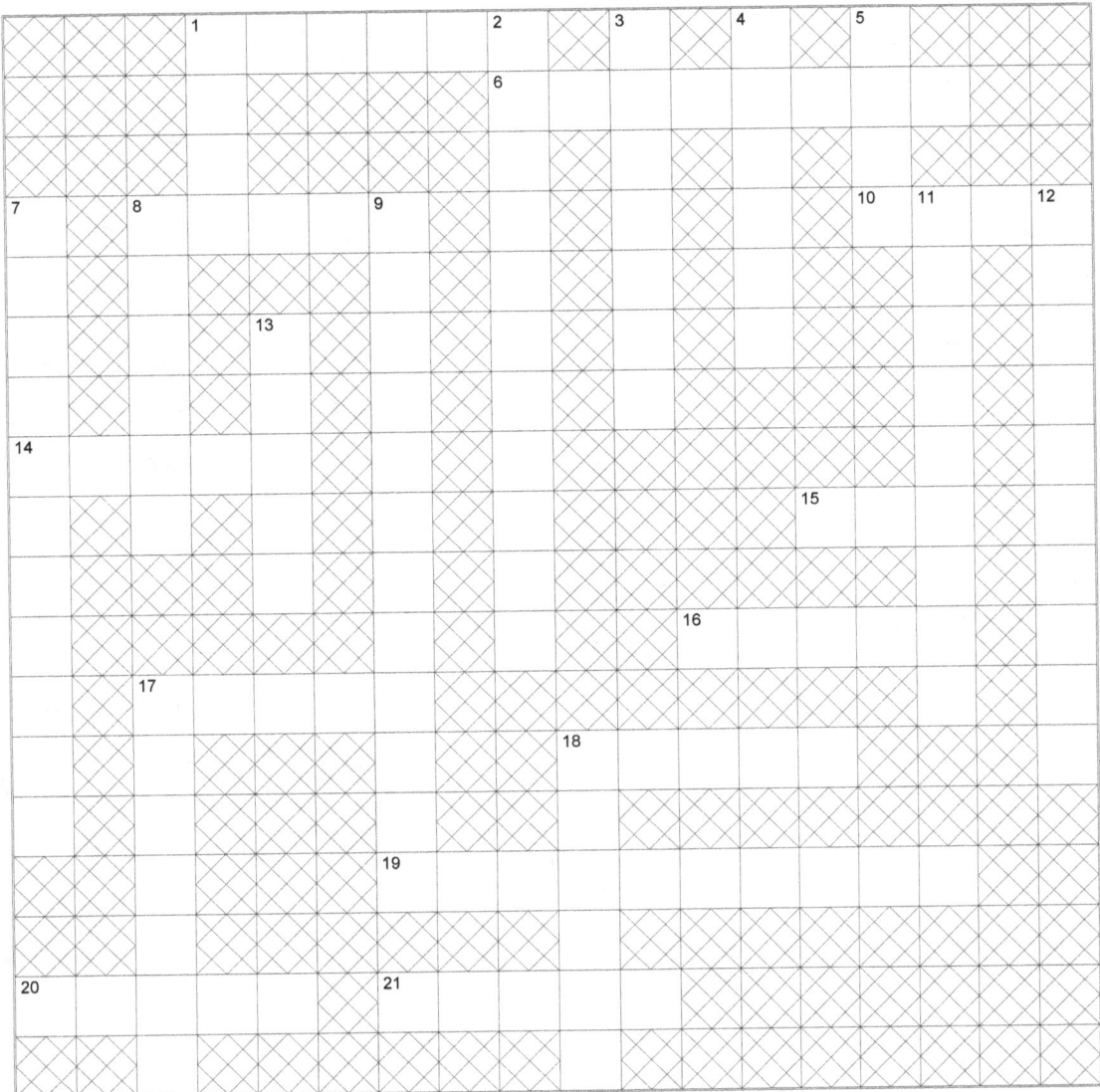

Across
1. Gulliver's friend in Lagado
6. Gulliver's name in Brobdingnag
8. None done in land of Houyhnhnms
10. Proper way to break them was disputed in Lilliput
14. Only Europeans allowed in Japan
15. Currently in power in Lilliput: ___ Heels
16. Man's worst vice, according to Gulliver
17. Worst crime in Lilliput
18. Unpleasant company for Gulliver: ___ of Honor
19. Continent under Laputa
20. Houyhnhnm council meeting: ___ Assembly
21. Fond of Gulliver's company in Brobdingnag

Down
1. Gulliver's wife
2. Articles of treason against Gulliver
3. Gulliver's home
4. Captain who found Gulliver near Blefuscu
5. Bird that carried Gulliver's box out to sea
7. Land of big people
8. Floating island
9. Governor here called forth dead persons
11. King of Brobdingnag refused this gift
12. Animal of Brobdingnag
13. Bestial man-like creature
17. Gulliver's enemy in Lilliput
18. Thought Gulliver was his young one

Gulliver's Travels Crossword 2 Answer Key

		1 M	U	N	O	D	2 I		3 E		4 B		5 K		
		A					6 M	A	N	N	I	K	I	N	
		R					P		G		D		T		
7 B	8 L	Y	I	N	9 G		E		L		D		10 E	11 G	12 S
R	A				L		A		A		L		U		P
O	P		13 Y		U		C		N		E		N		L
B	U		A		B		H		D				P		A
14 D	U	T	C	H		B		M					O		C
I			A			O		D				15 L	O	W	K
N			H			O		U					D		N
G			O			B		T			16 P	R	I	D	E
N	17 F	R	A	U	D								R		U
A	L				R		18 M	A	I	D	S				C
G	I				I		O								K
	M				19 B	A	L	N	I	B	A	R	B	I	
	N						K								
20 G	R	A	N	D		21 Q	U	E	E	N					
	P						Y								

Across
1. Gulliver's friend in Lagado
6. Gulliver's name in Brobdingnag
8. None done in land of Houyhnhnms
10. Proper way to break them was disputed in Lilliput
14. Only Europeans allowed in Japan
15. Currently in power in Lilliput: ___ Heels
16. Man's worst vice, according to Gulliver
17. Worst crime in Lilliput
18. Unpleasant company for Gulliver: ___ of Honor
19. Continent under Laputa
20. Houyhnhnm council meeting: ___ Assembly
21. Fond of Gulliver's company in Brobdingnag

Down
1. Gulliver's wife
2. Articles of treason against Gulliver
3. Gulliver's home
4. Captain who found Gulliver near Blefuscu
5. Bird that carried Gulliver's box out to sea
7. Land of big people
8. Floating island
9. Governor here called forth dead persons
11. King of Brobdingnag refused this gift
12. Animal of Brobdingnag
13. Bestial man-like creature
17. Gulliver's enemy in Lilliput
18. Thought Gulliver was his young one

Gulliver's Travels Crossword 3

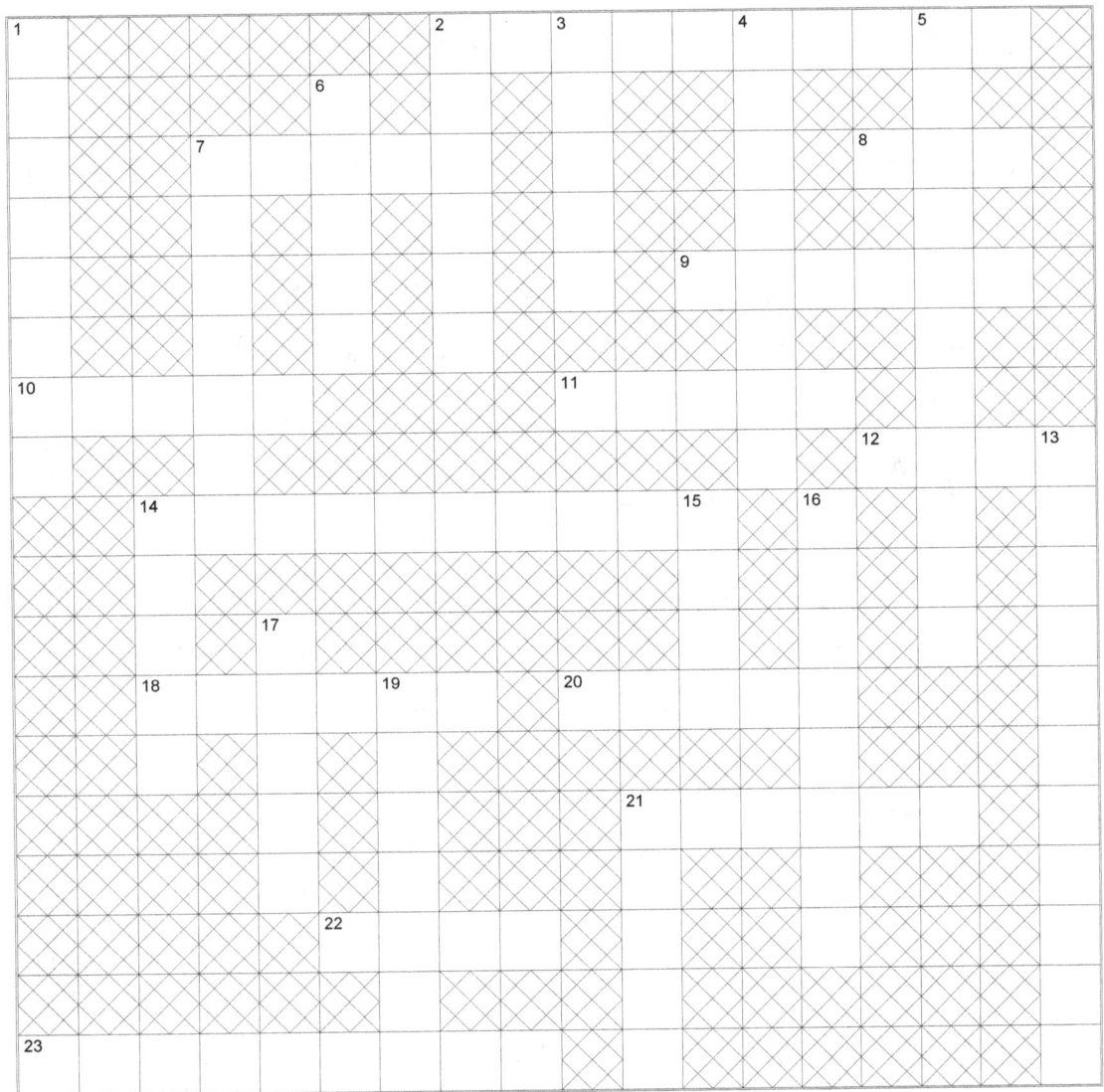

Across
2. Continent under Laputa
7. Worst crime in Lilliput
8. Currently in power in Lilliput: ___ Heels
9. Gulliver's friend in Lagado
10. Houyhnhnm council meeting: ___ Assembly
11. Only Europeans allowed in Japan
12. Proper way to break them was disputed in Lilliput
14. Animal of Brobdingnag
18. Displayed Gulliver to make money
20. Fond of Gulliver's company in Brobdingnag
21. Thought Gulliver was his young one
22. Gulliver's wife
23. King of Brobdingnag refused this gift

Down
1. Gulliver licked the king's floor here
2. Captain who found Gulliver near Blefuscu
3. None done in land of Houyhnhnms
4. Land of enemies of Lilliput
5. Land of big people
6. Bestial man-like creature
7. Gulliver's enemy in Lilliput
13. People who live forever
14. Author of GULLIVER'S TRAVELS
15. Bird that carried Gulliver's box out to sea
16. Gulliver's name in Brobdingnag
17. Man's worst vice, according to Gulliver
19. Gulliver's home
21. Unpleasant company for Gulliver: ___ of Honor

Gulliver's Travels Crossword 3 Answer Key

¹L						²B	³L	N	I	⁴B	A	R	⁵B	I
U				⁶Y		I		Y		L			R	
G		⁷F	R	A	U	D		I		E		⁸L	O	W
G		L		H		D		N		F			B	
N		I		O		L		G		⁹M	U	N	O	D	I
A		M		O		E				S			I	
¹⁰G	R	A	N	D				¹¹D	U	T	C	H		N	
G		A								U		¹²E	G	G	¹³S
		¹⁴S	P	L	A	C	K	N	U	¹⁵C	K	¹⁶M		N		T
		W								I		A		A		R
		I		¹⁷P						T		N		G		U
		¹⁸F	A	R	M	¹⁹E	R		²⁰Q	U	E	E	N			L
		T		I		N				I						D
				D		G			²¹M	O	N	K	E	Y		B
				E		L			A			I				R
						²²M	A	R	Y			N				U
						N			D							G
²³G	U	N	P	O	W	D	E	R		S						S

Across
2. Continent under Laputa
7. Worst crime in Lilliput
8. Currently in power in Lilliput: ___ Heels
9. Gulliver's friend in Lagado
10. Houyhnhnm council meeting: ___ Assembly
11. Only Europeans allowed in Japan
12. Proper way to break them was disputed in Lilliput
14. Animal of Brobdingnag
18. Displayed Gulliver to make money
20. Fond of Gulliver's company in Brobdingnag
21. Thought Gulliver was his young one
22. Gulliver's wife
23. King of Brobdingnag refused this gift

Down
1. Gulliver licked the king's floor here
2. Captain who found Gulliver near Blefuscu
3. None done in land of Houyhnhnms
4. Land of enemies of Lilliput
5. Land of big people
6. Bestial man-like creature
7. Gulliver's enemy in Lilliput
13. People who live forever
14. Author of GULLIVER'S TRAVELS
15. Bird that carried Gulliver's box out to sea
16. Gulliver's name in Brobdingnag
17. Man's worst vice, according to Gulliver
19. Gulliver's home
21. Unpleasant company for Gulliver: ___ of Honor

Gulliver's Travels Crossword 4

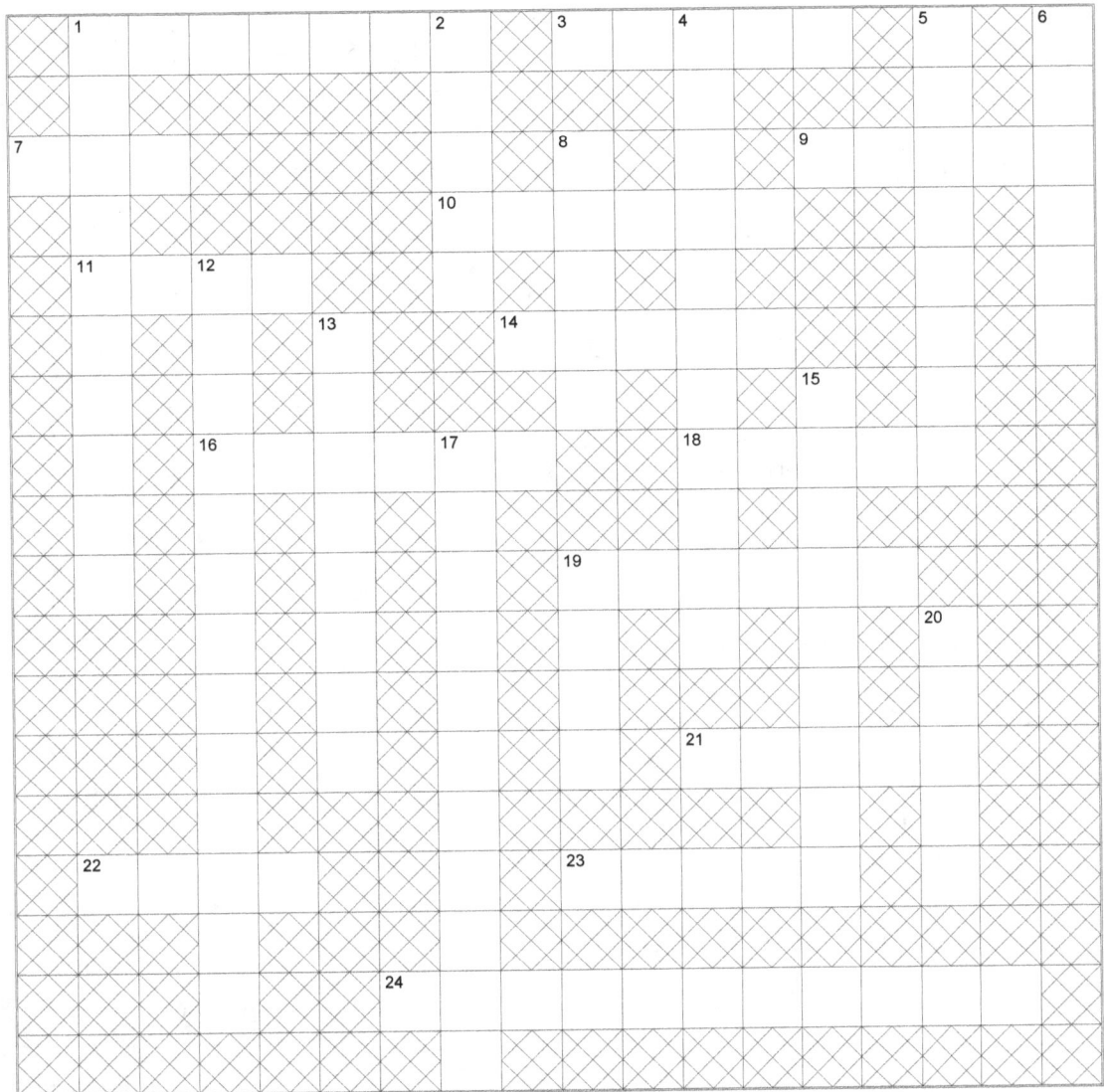

Across
1. Set Gulliver adrift in a sloop
3. None done in land of Houyhnhnms
7. Currently in power in Lilliput: ___ Heels
9. Houyhnhnm council meeting: ___ Assembly
10. Displayed Gulliver to make money
11. Proper way to break them was disputed in Lilliput
14. Only Europeans allowed in Japan
16. Thought Gulliver was his young one
18. Unpleasant company for Gulliver: ___ of Honor
19. Gulliver's friend in Lagado
21. Man's worst vice, according to Gulliver
22. Bird that carried Gulliver's box out to sea
23. Bestial man-like creature
24. People who live forever

Down
1. Academy trying new methods
2. Author of GULLIVER'S TRAVELS
4. Articles of treason against Gulliver
5. Servants who hit their masters
6. Captain who found Gulliver near Blefuscu
8. Worst crime in Lilliput
12. Gulliver's 'little nurse'
13. Gulliver's name in Brobdingnag
15. Rebellious city in Laputa
17. Houyhnhnm plan for Yahoos
19. Gulliver's wife
20. Fond of Gulliver's company in Brobdingnag

Gulliver's Travels Crossword 4 Answer Key

		1 P	I	R	A	T	E	2 S		3 L		4 Y	I	N	G		5 F		6 B
		R						W				M					L		I
7 L	O	W						I		8 F		P		9 G	R	A	N	D
		J						10 F	A	R	M	E	R				P		D
		11 E	G	12 G	S			T		A		A					P		L
		C		L		13 M		14 D	U	T	C	H		15 L			E		E
		T		U		A			D			H		L			R		
		O		16 M	O	N	K	17 E	Y			18 M	A	I	D	S			
		R		D		N		X				E		N					
		S		A		I		T		19 M	U	N	O	D	I				
				L		K		E		A		T		A			20 Q		
				C		I		R		R		A		L			U		
				L		N		M		Y		21 P	R	I	D	E			
				I				I						N			E		
		22 K	I	T	E			N		23 Y	A	H	O	O			N		
				C				A											
				H		24 S	T	R	U	L	D	B	R	U	G	S			
						E													

Across
1. Set Gulliver adrift in a sloop
3. None done in land of Houyhnhnms
7. Currently in power in Lilliput: ___ Heels
9. Houyhnhnm council meeting: ___ Assembly
10. Displayed Gulliver to make money
11. Proper way to break them was disputed in Lilliput
14. Only Europeans allowed in Japan
16. Thought Gulliver was his young one
18. Unpleasant company for Gulliver: ___ of Honor
19. Gulliver's friend in Lagado
21. Man's worst vice, according to Gulliver
22. Bird that carried Gulliver's box out to sea
23. Bestial man-like creature
24. People who live forever

Down
1. Academy trying new methods
2. Author of GULLIVER'S TRAVELS
4. Articles of treason against Gulliver
5. Servants who hit their masters
6. Captain who found Gulliver near Blefuscu
8. Worst crime in Lilliput
12. Gulliver's 'little nurse'
13. Gulliver's name in Brobdingnag
15. Rebellious city in Laputa
17. Houyhnhnm plan for Yahoos
19. Gulliver's wife
20. Fond of Gulliver's company in Brobdingnag

Gulliver's Travels

MUNODI	FRAUD	LILLIPUT	FLAPPERS	LOW
EGGS	GLUBBDUBDRIB	ENGLAND	SWIFT	SPLACKNUCK
PIRATES	LUGGNAGG	FREE SPACE	DUTCH	GLUMDALCLITCH
BALNIBARBI	HOUYHNHNMS	YAHOO	STRULDBRUGS	PROJECTORS
FARMER	MANNIKIN	HOPEWELL	KITE	BLEFUSCU

Gulliver's Travels

GUNPOWDER	GRAND	EXTERMINATE	MARY	LAPUTA
GULLIVER	MAIDS	FLIMNAP	BIDDLE	LYING
MONKEY	LINDALINO	FREE SPACE	IMPEACHMENT	BROBDINGNAG
BLEFUSCU	KITE	HOPEWELL	MANNIKIN	FARMER
PROJECTORS	STRULDBRUGS	YAHOO	HOUYHNHNMS	BALNIBARBI

Gulliver's Travels

BROBDINGNAG	MONKEY	LUGGNAGG	LAPUTA	GUNPOWDER
LINDALINO	BALNIBARBI	FLAPPERS	ENGLAND	MUNODI
PIRATES	BIDDLE	FREE SPACE	LYING	FRAUD
HOPEWELL	QUEEN	MANNIKIN	PROJECTORS	GLUMDALCLITCH
FARMER	GRAND	SWIFT	MARY	EXTERMINATE

Gulliver's Travels

GULLIVER	KITE	LILLIPUT	BLEFUSCU	IMPEACHMENT
EGGS	FLIMNAP	MAIDS	HOUYHNHNMS	GLUBBDUBDRIB
DUTCH	PRIDE	FREE SPACE	STRULDBRUGS	SPLACKNUCK
EXTERMINATE	MARY	SWIFT	GRAND	FARMER
GLUMDALCLITCH	PROJECTORS	MANNIKIN	QUEEN	HOPEWELL

Gulliver's Travels

DUTCH	GLUMDALCLITCH	MAIDS	YAHOO	PIRATES
EGGS	HOPEWELL	GUNPOWDER	BROBDINGNAG	MONKEY
FLAPPERS	HOUYHNHNMS	FREE SPACE	GRAND	FRAUD
LOW	FARMER	GULLIVER	LINDALINO	BLEFUSCU
BIDDLE	STRULDBRUGS	LILLIPUT	SWIFT	FLIMNAP

Gulliver's Travels

IMPEACHMENT	QUEEN	KITE	GLUBBDUBDRIB	LAPUTA
EXTERMINATE	SPLACKNUCK	MANNIKIN	MUNODI	MARY
PROJECTORS	BALNIBARBI	FREE SPACE	LUGGNAGG	PRIDE
FLIMNAP	SWIFT	LILLIPUT	STRULDBRUGS	BIDDLE
BLEFUSCU	LINDALINO	GULLIVER	FARMER	LOW

Gulliver's Travels

YAHOO	SPLACKNUCK	EGGS	FARMER	MAIDS
BLEFUSCU	BALNIBARBI	MONKEY	SWIFT	KITE
LILLIPUT	GLUBBDUBDRIB	FREE SPACE	LUGGNAGG	DUTCH
GULLIVER	GUNPOWDER	STRULDBRUGS	FRAUD	ENGLAND
LAPUTA	MARY	QUEEN	LINDALINO	FLIMNAP

Gulliver's Travels

GRAND	LOW	HOUYHNHNMS	GLUMDALCLITCH	EXTERMINATE
PROJECTORS	MANNIKIN	BIDDLE	BROBDINGNAG	MUNODI
HOPEWELL	PRIDE	FREE SPACE	FLAPPERS	IMPEACHMENT
FLIMNAP	LINDALINO	QUEEN	MARY	LAPUTA
ENGLAND	FRAUD	STRULDBRUGS	GUNPOWDER	GULLIVER

Gulliver's Travels

IMPEACHMENT	EGGS	MANNIKIN	LYING	LOW
SPLACKNUCK	BLEFUSCU	FLAPPERS	ENGLAND	HOUYHNHNMS
MARY	QUEEN	FREE SPACE	LUGGNAGG	FRAUD
FLIMNAP	EXTERMINATE	BIDDLE	LAPUTA	LINDALINO
BALNIBARBI	GULLIVER	YAHOO	STRULDBRUGS	MAIDS

Gulliver's Travels

GLUBBDUBDRIB	PIRATES	SWIFT	PROJECTORS	LILLIPUT
FARMER	KITE	MUNODI	MONKEY	HOPEWELL
GUNPOWDER	PRIDE	FREE SPACE	GLUMDALCLITCH	GRAND
MAIDS	STRULDBRUGS	YAHOO	GULLIVER	BALNIBARBI
LINDALINO	LAPUTA	BIDDLE	EXTERMINATE	FLIMNAP

Gulliver's Travels

HOPEWELL	HOUYHNHNMS	STRULDBRUGS	LAPUTA	SWIFT
LUGGNAGG	FRAUD	GRAND	LILLIPUT	FARMER
EXTERMINATE	YAHOO	FREE SPACE	ENGLAND	DUTCH
MARY	GLUMDALCLITCH	MONKEY	MAIDS	PIRATES
BROBDINGNAG	FLAPPERS	IMPEACHMENT	BALNIBARBI	SPLACKNUCK

Gulliver's Travels

LYING	LOW	GUNPOWDER	BIDDLE	QUEEN
KITE	MANNIKIN	GULLIVER	MUNODI	FLIMNAP
PRIDE	GLUBBDUBDRIB	FREE SPACE	PROJECTORS	BLEFUSCU
SPLACKNUCK	BALNIBARBI	IMPEACHMENT	FLAPPERS	BROBDINGNAG
PIRATES	MAIDS	MONKEY	GLUMDALCLITCH	MARY

Gulliver's Travels

DUTCH	FRAUD	GLUBBDUBDRIB	FLAPPERS	ENGLAND
BALNIBARBI	HOPEWELL	MAIDS	BIDDLE	GULLIVER
GRAND	LUGGNAGG	FREE SPACE	STRULDBRUGS	MUNODI
BROBDINGNAG	BLEFUSCU	FARMER	EXTERMINATE	GUNPOWDER
QUEEN	PRIDE	MANNIKIN	GLUMDALCLITCH	KITE

Gulliver's Travels

HOUYHNHNMS	MARY	PIRATES	YAHOO	SWIFT
LOW	LAPUTA	SPLACKNUCK	IMPEACHMENT	PROJECTORS
LYING	EGGS	FREE SPACE	FLIMNAP	MONKEY
KITE	GLUMDALCLITCH	MANNIKIN	PRIDE	QUEEN
GUNPOWDER	EXTERMINATE	FARMER	BLEFUSCU	BROBDINGNAG

Gulliver's Travels

LYING	MAIDS	MUNODI	BIDDLE	PRIDE
BROBDINGNAG	YAHOO	GUNPOWDER	FLAPPERS	LINDALINO
LUGGNAGG	STRULDBRUGS	FREE SPACE	SPLACKNUCK	FRAUD
HOUYHNHNMS	GULLIVER	IMPEACHMENT	BALNIBARBI	PIRATES
HOPEWELL	SWIFT	LILLIPUT	KITE	MONKEY

Gulliver's Travels

FARMER	LAPUTA	FLIMNAP	LOW	EGGS
MANNIKIN	MARY	GLUMDALCLITCH	QUEEN	PROJECTORS
ENGLAND	BLEFUSCU	FREE SPACE	GLUBBDUBDRIB	GRAND
MONKEY	KITE	LILLIPUT	SWIFT	HOPEWELL
PIRATES	BALNIBARBI	IMPEACHMENT	GULLIVER	HOUYHNHNMS

Gulliver's Travels

YAHOO	BLEFUSCU	SWIFT	GLUBBDUBDRIB	LAPUTA
STRULDBRUGS	MUNODI	LILLIPUT	GULLIVER	FARMER
FRAUD	IMPEACHMENT	FREE SPACE	BALNIBARBI	PRIDE
GLUMDALCLITCH	MONKEY	LYING	SPLACKNUCK	LOW
KITE	FLAPPERS	HOPEWELL	PIRATES	LUGGNAGG

Gulliver's Travels

PROJECTORS	BROBDINGNAG	GRAND	QUEEN	EXTERMINATE
EGGS	MAIDS	MARY	GUNPOWDER	LINDALINO
DUTCH	HOUYHNHNMS	FREE SPACE	ENGLAND	MANNIKIN
LUGGNAGG	PIRATES	HOPEWELL	FLAPPERS	KITE
LOW	SPLACKNUCK	LYING	MONKEY	GLUMDALCLITCH

Gulliver's Travels

STRULDBRUGS	EXTERMINATE	FLIMNAP	MAIDS	LAPUTA
HOUYHNHNMS	FARMER	IMPEACHMENT	HOPEWELL	QUEEN
SPLACKNUCK	FRAUD	FREE SPACE	LYING	GUNPOWDER
PROJECTORS	GLUBBDUBDRIB	BROBDINGNAG	MANNIKIN	BIDDLE
GRAND	MARY	BALNIBARBI	EGGS	KITE

Gulliver's Travels

SWIFT	MUNODI	PIRATES	LILLIPUT	PRIDE
MONKEY	FLAPPERS	LINDALINO	YAHOO	GULLIVER
LOW	ENGLAND	FREE SPACE	BLEFUSCU	GLUMDALCLITCH
KITE	EGGS	BALNIBARBI	MARY	GRAND
BIDDLE	MANNIKIN	BROBDINGNAG	GLUBBDUBDRIB	PROJECTORS

Gulliver's Travels

MARY	GLUMDALCLITCH	BIDDLE	ENGLAND	BALNIBARBI
IMPEACHMENT	BLEFUSCU	MAIDS	GRAND	GUNPOWDER
LUGGNAGG	HOPEWELL	FREE SPACE	PIRATES	DUTCH
FLIMNAP	QUEEN	FLAPPERS	LAPUTA	LINDALINO
KITE	LILLIPUT	STRULDBRUGS	LOW	HOUYHNHNMS

Gulliver's Travels

PRIDE	EXTERMINATE	SPLACKNUCK	BROBDINGNAG	YAHOO
GULLIVER	EGGS	GLUBBDUBDRIB	FRAUD	PROJECTORS
MANNIKIN	LYING	FREE SPACE	MONKEY	SWIFT
HOUYHNHNMS	LOW	STRULDBRUGS	LILLIPUT	KITE
LINDALINO	LAPUTA	FLAPPERS	QUEEN	FLIMNAP

Gulliver's Travels

FLIMNAP	BROBDINGNAG	LYING	PRIDE	LUGGNAGG
STRULDBRUGS	QUEEN	FARMER	GLUMDALCLITCH	GULLIVER
ENGLAND	BALNIBARBI	FREE SPACE	MANNIKIN	PROJECTORS
LILLIPUT	FRAUD	HOUYHNHNMS	KITE	MONKEY
YAHOO	HOPEWELL	MARY	FLAPPERS	SWIFT

Gulliver's Travels

EGGS	GLUBBDUBDRIB	PIRATES	SPLACKNUCK	BIDDLE
LAPUTA	LINDALINO	MAIDS	GRAND	LOW
IMPEACHMENT	EXTERMINATE	FREE SPACE	GUNPOWDER	BLEFUSCU
SWIFT	FLAPPERS	MARY	HOPEWELL	YAHOO
MONKEY	KITE	HOUYHNHNMS	FRAUD	LILLIPUT

Gulliver's Travels

KITE	EXTERMINATE	PROJECTORS	GLUBBDUBDRIB	FLAPPERS
BALNIBARBI	GRAND	GULLIVER	GLUMDALCLITCH	FRAUD
DUTCH	GUNPOWDER	FREE SPACE	SPLACKNUCK	MUNODI
HOUYHNHNMS	IMPEACHMENT	MONKEY	BROBDINGNAG	BLEFUSCU
BIDDLE	FLIMNAP	MAIDS	PRIDE	STRULDBRUGS

Gulliver's Travels

QUEEN	LINDALINO	FARMER	LAPUTA	SWIFT
LUGGNAGG	EGGS	LOW	MARY	YAHOO
ENGLAND	LYING	FREE SPACE	PIRATES	LILLIPUT
STRULDBRUGS	PRIDE	MAIDS	FLIMNAP	BIDDLE
BLEFUSCU	BROBDINGNAG	MONKEY	IMPEACHMENT	HOUYHNHNMS

Gulliver's Travels

LILLIPUT	LYING	GULLIVER	MANNIKIN	QUEEN
MAIDS	PIRATES	GUNPOWDER	HOPEWELL	ENGLAND
MUNODI	IMPEACHMENT	FREE SPACE	SWIFT	BIDDLE
KITE	STRULDBRUGS	FARMER	SPLACKNUCK	YAHOO
EGGS	MARY	BROBDINGNAG	LUGGNAGG	BALNIBARBI

Gulliver's Travels

GLUBBDUBDRIB	GRAND	GLUMDALCLITCH	LAPUTA	EXTERMINATE
DUTCH	MONKEY	BLEFUSCU	HOUYHNHNMS	FLIMNAP
FRAUD	LINDALINO	FREE SPACE	PRIDE	FLAPPERS
BALNIBARBI	LUGGNAGG	BROBDINGNAG	MARY	EGGS
YAHOO	SPLACKNUCK	FARMER	STRULDBRUGS	KITE

Gulliver's Travels

PIRATES	IMPEACHMENT	BLEFUSCU	GUNPOWDER	MANNIKIN
LUGGNAGG	GLUMDALCLITCH	SWIFT	DUTCH	HOUYHNHNMS
YAHOO	LILLIPUT	FREE SPACE	MAIDS	GULLIVER
LOW	EXTERMINATE	GLUBBDUBDRIB	PRIDE	QUEEN
BROBDINGNAG	EGGS	FRAUD	PROJECTORS	KITE

Gulliver's Travels

HOPEWELL	LYING	MUNODI	BIDDLE	LINDALINO
ENGLAND	FARMER	SPLACKNUCK	STRULDBRUGS	GRAND
FLAPPERS	BALNIBARBI	FREE SPACE	MONKEY	FLIMNAP
KITE	PROJECTORS	FRAUD	EGGS	BROBDINGNAG
QUEEN	PRIDE	GLUBBDUBDRIB	EXTERMINATE	LOW

Gulliver's Travels

FLAPPERS	HOUYHNHNMS	HOPEWELL	FARMER	LAPUTA
IMPEACHMENT	MANNIKIN	MAIDS	PRIDE	BLEFUSCU
QUEEN	FRAUD	FREE SPACE	DUTCH	MUNODI
KITE	LYING	STRULDBRUGS	YAHOO	PROJECTORS
LINDALINO	LUGGNAGG	BALNIBARBI	BROBDINGNAG	MARY

Gulliver's Travels

LOW	GRAND	LILLIPUT	GUNPOWDER	BIDDLE
ENGLAND	GLUMDALCLITCH	FLIMNAP	GULLIVER	MONKEY
PIRATES	EXTERMINATE	FREE SPACE	EGGS	SWIFT
MARY	BROBDINGNAG	BALNIBARBI	LUGGNAGG	LINDALINO
PROJECTORS	YAHOO	STRULDBRUGS	LYING	KITE

Gulliver's Travels Vocabulary Word List

No.	Word	Clue/Definition
1.	ACCOUTERED	Equipped with trappings, accessories
2.	ADAMANT	Impenetrably hard
3.	ALACRITY	Briskness; cheerful readiness
4.	ALLUSION	Indirect reference
5.	ANIMOSITIES	Bitter hostilities; hatred
6.	APPELLATION	Act of naming; act of appealing; a name or title
7.	AUDITOR	One authorized to audit accounts
8.	BATTALIA	An army in battle array or on the march
9.	CADENCE	Beat of any rhythmical movement
10.	CANDOUR	Sincerity; honesty; purity of character
11.	CIRCUMLOCUTIONS	Speaking in a round about way; use of many words when a few would work
12.	CIRCUMSPECTION	Caution; heedfulness
13.	CLEMENCY	Mercy
14.	COMELINESS	Pleasing appearance
15.	COMMODIOUS	Convenient or satisfactory for the purpose; spacious, roomy
16.	CONFEDERACY	League or alliance
17.	CONJECTURE	Infer from inconclusive evidence
18.	CONSUMMATE	Complete or perfect; of the highest quality
19.	COPSE	Wood or thicket of small trees and bushes
20.	COUNTENANCE	Face; expression on a face
21.	DEBAUCHED	Caused to forsake allegiance
22.	DECLIVITY	Sloping downward
23.	DELINEATE	Portray in words; describe; sketch or trace in outline
24.	DEPOSE	Give sworn testimony; to lay aside; remove from office
25.	DIMINUTIVE	Small; tiny
26.	DISAPPROBATION	Disapproval
27.	DISCOURSE	Conversation; formal discussion as a dissertation or sermon
28.	DISDAIN	Feeling, attitude, or show of scornful superiority
29.	DIURNAL	Pertaining to day
30.	EDIFICE	A building, especially one of large size or imposing appearance
31.	ERUDITION	Learning; scholarship; knowledge
32.	ESPALIER	Trellis or framework on which trees or shrubs are trained to grow in a flattened form
33.	EXHORTATION	Act of giving urgent advice or admonition as to conduct
34.	EXPEDIENT	Conducive to a result
35.	EXPOSTULATE	Reason earnestly with someone
36.	EXTENUATIONS	Partial excuses; serve to make less serious
37.	FELICITY	High degree of happiness; singular grace, as of manner
38.	FOPPERIES	Manners, etc. of a foolish person
39.	GROVELLING	Without dignity or aspirations
40.	HERMETICALLY	Closed as to be air tight
41.	HOGSHEAD	Large cask
42.	IGNOMINIOUS	Deserving shame or disgrace
43.	IGNOMINY	Dishonor; infamy
44.	IMPEACHMENT	Discrediting or degrading
45.	IMPUTED	Attributed to
46.	INADVERTENCE	Mistake or oversight; something not intentional
47.	INIMITABLE	Cannot be imitated or reproduced; matchless
48.	INSATIABLE	Not able to be satisfied

Gulliver's Travels Vocabulary Word List

No. Word	Clue/Definition
49. INSIPID	Dull; without interesting qualities
50. INSUPERABLE	Unable to be overcome
51. INTERPOSITION	Act of putting between; intervention on behalf of a person
52. INTREPIDITY	Courage; fearlessness
53. INVIOLABLE	Not to be violated; treated as if sacred
54. KITE	Predatory bird having a long, forked tail
55. LEAGUES	Units of distance, each equal to 3 miles
56. LICENTIOUSNESS	Unrestrained by law or morality; beyond proper limits
57. MASTIFF	Large dog of ancient breed
58. MAXIM	Axiom; an expression of a general truth
59. MIZZEN	Sail near the stern of a 3-masted vessel
60. NECROMANCY	Magic; conjuration
61. ODIOUS	Hateful or detestable; obnoxious
62. ORTHOGRAPHY	Dealing with letters and spelling
63. PANDERISM	Catering to the baser passions of others
64. PARITY	Equality
65. PERUSED	Read; scrutinized
66. POSTERITY	Descendants; succeeding generations
67. PRODIGIOUS	Extraordinary size, amount
68. PROGNOSTICS	Forecasting what is to come
69. PROPAGATE	Cause animals to multiply or breed
70. PROPENSITY	Natural inclination or tendency
71. PROVOCATIVE	A stimulant
72. PURSUANT	Proceeding from and conformable to; in accordance with
73. QUADRANT	A square; navigation instrument
74. RAILLERY	Banter; good-humored ridicule
75. RECAPITULATION	Summary or repeating
76. RECLUSE	One who lives withdrawn from the world
77. RECOMPENSED	Paid; made compensation for
78. REDUNDANT	Needlessly repetitive
79. RUDIMENTS	Beginnings; first attempts; elementary
80. SCHISMS	Divisions into mutually opposed parties
81. SCROFULOUS	Swelling of lymphatic glands
82. SCRUPULOUS	Carefully conforming to the dictates of conscience
83. SORREL	Horse of reddish-brown color
84. TRENCHER	Flat piece of wood on which meat is carved and served
85. VEHEMENCE	Characterized by violence of feeling or endeavor; passion
86. VERNAL	Having to do with spring
87. VINDICATED	Set free; defended; avenged
88. VOGUE	Fashion at a particular time
89. ZENITH	Highest point; culmination

Copyrighted

Gulliver's Travels Vocabulary Fill In The Blank 1

_____ 1. Feeling, attitude, or show of scornful superiority

_____ 2. Units of distance, each equal to 3 miles

_____ 3. Briskness; cheerful readiness

_____ 4. Deserving shame or disgrace

_____ 5. Descendants; succeeding generations

_____ 6. Horse of reddish-brown color

_____ 7. A square; navigation instrument

_____ 8. Swelling of lymphatic glands

_____ 9. Bitter hostilities; hatred

_____ 10. Highest point; culmination

_____ 11. Disapproval

_____ 12. Caused to forsake allegiance

_____ 13. Pleasing appearance

_____ 14. Discrediting or degrading

_____ 15. Sincerity; honesty; purity of character

_____ 16. Needlessly repetitive

_____ 17. Extraordinary size, amount

_____ 18. Trellis or framework on which trees or shrubs are trained to grow in a flattened form

_____ 19. Small; tiny

_____ 20. Act of putting between; intervention on behalf of a person

Gulliver's Travels Vocabulary Fill In The Blank 1 Answer Key

DISDAIN	1.	Feeling, attitude, or show of scornful superiority
LEAGUES	2.	Units of distance, each equal to 3 miles
ALACRITY	3.	Briskness; cheerful readiness
IGNOMINIOUS	4.	Deserving shame or disgrace
POSTERITY	5.	Descendants; succeeding generations
SORREL	6.	Horse of reddish-brown color
QUADRANT	7.	A square; navigation instrument
SCROFULOUS	8.	Swelling of lymphatic glands
ANIMOSITIES	9.	Bitter hostilities; hatred
ZENITH	10.	Highest point; culmination
DISAPPROBATION	11.	Disapproval
DEBAUCHED	12.	Caused to forsake allegiance
COMELINESS	13.	Pleasing appearance
IMPEACHMENT	14.	Discrediting or degrading
CANDOUR	15.	Sincerity; honesty; purity of character
REDUNDANT	16.	Needlessly repetitive
PRODIGIOUS	17.	Extraordinary size, amount
ESPALIER	18.	Trellis or framework on which trees or shrubs are trained to grow in a flattened form
DIMINUTIVE	19.	Small; tiny
INTERPOSITION	20.	Act of putting between; intervention on behalf of a person

Gulliver's Travels Vocabulary Fill In The Blank 2

_____ 1. Wood or thicket of small trees and bushes

_____ 2. Equality

_____ 3. Bitter hostilities; hatred

_____ 4. Manners, etc. of a foolish person

_____ 5. Mercy

_____ 6. Infer from inconclusive evidence

_____ 7. Deserving shame or disgrace

_____ 8. Read; scrutinized

_____ 9. Sloping downward

_____ 10. Fashion at a particular time

_____ 11. Swelling of lymphatic glands

_____ 12. Banter; good-humored ridicule

_____ 13. Portray in words; describe; sketch or trace in outline

_____ 14. Divisions into mutually opposed parties

_____ 15. Set free; defended; avenged

_____ 16. Units of distance, each equal to 3 miles

_____ 17. Paid; made compensation for

_____ 18. Courage; fearlessness

_____ 19. Large cask

_____ 20. Unrestrained by law or morality; beyond proper limits

Gulliver's Travels Vocabulary Fill In The Blank 2 Answer Key

COPSE	1. Wood or thicket of small trees and bushes
PARITY	2. Equality
ANIMOSITIES	3. Bitter hostilities; hatred
FOPPERIES	4. Manners, etc. of a foolish person
CLEMENCY	5. Mercy
CONJECTURE	6. Infer from inconclusive evidence
IGNOMINIOUS	7. Deserving shame or disgrace
PERUSED	8. Read; scrutinized
DECLIVITY	9. Sloping downward
VOGUE	10. Fashion at a particular time
SCROFULOUS	11. Swelling of lymphatic glands
RAILLERY	12. Banter; good-humored ridicule
DELINEATE	13. Portray in words; describe; sketch or trace in outline
SCHISMS	14. Divisions into mutually opposed parties
VINDICATED	15. Set free; defended; avenged
LEAGUES	16. Units of distance, each equal to 3 miles
RECOMPENSED	17. Paid; made compensation for
INTREPIDITY	18. Courage; fearlessness
HOGSHEAD	19. Large cask
LICENTIOUSNESS	20. Unrestrained by law or morality; beyond proper limits

Gulliver's Travels Vocabulary Fill In The Blank 3

_____ 1. Attributed to

_____ 2. Summary or repeating

_____ 3. Fashion at a particular time

_____ 4. Characterized by violence of feeling or endeavor; passion

_____ 5. Conducive to a result

_____ 6. Not to be violated; treated as if sacred

_____ 7. Feeling, attitude, or show of scornful superiority

_____ 8. Unrestrained by law or morality; beyond proper limits

_____ 9. Mistake or oversight; something not intentional

_____ 10. Learning; scholarship; knowledge

_____ 11. Beginnings; first attempts; elementary

_____ 12. Natural inclination or tendency

_____ 13. League or alliance

_____ 14. Equipped with trappings, accessories

_____ 15. Act of putting between; intervention on behalf of a person

_____ 16. High degree of happiness; singular grace, as of manner

_____ 17. Briskness; cheerful readiness

_____ 18. Carefully conforming to the dictates of conscience

_____ 19. Descendants; succeeding generations

_____ 20. Catering to the baser passions of others

Gulliver's Travels Vocabulary Fill In The Blank 3 Answer Key

IMPUTED	1. Attributed to
RECAPITULATION	2. Summary or repeating
VOGUE	3. Fashion at a particular time
VEHEMENCE	4. Characterized by violence of feeling or endeavor; passion
EXPEDIENT	5. Conducive to a result
INVIOLABLE	6. Not to be violated; treated as if sacred
DISDAIN	7. Feeling, attitude, or show of scornful superiority
LICENTIOUSNESS	8. Unrestrained by law or morality; beyond proper limits
INADVERTENCE	9. Mistake or oversight; something not intentional
ERUDITION	10. Learning; scholarship; knowledge
RUDIMENTS	11. Beginnings; first attempts; elementary
PROPENSITY	12. Natural inclination or tendency
CONFEDERACY	13. League or alliance
ACCOUTERED	14. Equipped with trappings, accessories
INTERPOSITION	15. Act of putting between; intervention on behalf of a person
FELICITY	16. High degree of happiness; singular grace, as of manner
ALACRITY	17. Briskness; cheerful readiness
SCRUPULOUS	18. Carefully conforming to the dictates of conscience
POSTERITY	19. Descendants; succeeding generations
PANDERISM	20. Catering to the baser passions of others

Gulliver's Travels Vocabulary Fill In The Blank 4

1. Magic; conjuration
2. Discrediting or degrading
3. Fashion at a particular time
4. Forecasting what is to come
5. Having to do with spring
6. Units of distance, each equal to 3 miles
7. Convenient or satisfactory for the purpose; spacious, roomy
8. Trellis or framework on which trees or shrubs are trained to grow in a flattened form
9. Bitter hostilities; hatred
10. Indirect reference
11. Speaking in a round about way; use of many words when a few would work
12. An army in battle array or on the march
13. Portray in words; describe; sketch or trace in outline
14. One authorized to audit accounts
15. Predatory bird having a long, forked tail
16. Axiom; an expression of a general truth
17. Wood or thicket of small trees and bushes
18. High degree of happiness; singular grace, as of manner
19. Courage; fearlessness
20. Hateful or detestable; obnoxious

Gulliver's Travels Vocabulary Fill In The Blank 4 Answer Key

NECROMANCY	1. Magic; conjuration
IMPEACHMENT	2. Discrediting or degrading
VOGUE	3. Fashion at a particular time
PROGNOSTICS	4. Forecasting what is to come
VERNAL	5. Having to do with spring
LEAGUES	6. Units of distance, each equal to 3 miles
COMMODIOUS	7. Convenient or satisfactory for the purpose; spacious, roomy
ESPALIER	8. Trellis or framework on which trees or shrubs are trained to grow in a flattened form
ANIMOSITIES	9. Bitter hostilities; hatred
ALLUSION	10. Indirect reference
CIRCUMLOCUTIONS	11. Speaking in a round about way; use of many words when a few would work
BATTALIA	12. An army in battle array or on the march
DELINEATE	13. Portray in words; describe; sketch or trace in outline
AUDITOR	14. One authorized to audit accounts
KITE	15. Predatory bird having a long, forked tail
MAXIM	16. Axiom; an expression of a general truth
COPSE	17. Wood or thicket of small trees and bushes
FELICITY	18. High degree of happiness; singular grace, as of manner
INTREPIDITY	19. Courage; fearlessness
ODIOUS	20. Hateful or detestable; obnoxious

Gulliver's Travels Vocabulary Matching 1

___ 1. ORTHOGRAPHY A. Face; expression on a face
___ 2. DEPOSE B. Read; scrutinized
___ 3. EXHORTATION C. Act of giving urgent advice or admonition as to conduct
___ 4. DIMINUTIVE D. High degree of happiness; singular grace, as of manner
___ 5. EXTENUATIONS E. Courage; fearlessness
___ 6. GROVELLING F. Catering to the baser passions of others
___ 7. ACCOUTERED G. Hateful or detestable; obnoxious
___ 8. DISCOURSE H. Without dignity or aspirations
___ 9. CADENCE I. Discrediting or degrading
___ 10. KITE J. Having to do with spring
___ 11. COMELINESS K. Give sworn testimony; to lay aside; remove from office
___ 12. PERUSED L. Convenient or satisfactory for the purpose; spacious, roomy
___ 13. FELICITY M. Conversation; formal discussion as a dissertation or sermon
___ 14. ODIOUS N. Equipped with trappings, accessories
___ 15. MIZZEN O. Wood or thicket of small trees and bushes
___ 16. RECOMPENSED P. Paid; made compensation for
___ 17. VERNAL Q. Sail near the stern of a 3-masted vessel
___ 18. PANDERISM R. Dealing with letters and spelling
___ 19. COPSE S. Small; tiny
___ 20. INTREPIDITY T. Impenetrably hard
___ 21. TRENCHER U. Beat of any rhythmical movement
___ 22. COUNTENANCE V. Predatory bird having a long, forked tail
___ 23. COMMODIOUS W. Partial excuses; serve to make less serious
___ 24. IMPEACHMENT X. Flat piece of wood on which meat is carved and served
___ 25. ADAMANT Y. Pleasing appearance

Gulliver's Travels Vocabulary Matching 1 Answer Key

R - 1. ORTHOGRAPHY
K - 2. DEPOSE
C - 3. EXHORTATION
S - 4. DIMINUTIVE
W - 5. EXTENUATIONS
H - 6. GROVELLING
N - 7. ACCOUTERED
M - 8. DISCOURSE
U - 9. CADENCE
V - 10. KITE
Y - 11. COMELINESS
B - 12. PERUSED
D - 13. FELICITY
G - 14. ODIOUS
Q - 15. MIZZEN
P - 16. RECOMPENSED
J - 17. VERNAL
F - 18. PANDERISM
O - 19. COPSE
E - 20. INTREPIDITY
X - 21. TRENCHER
A - 22. COUNTENANCE
L - 23. COMMODIOUS
I - 24. IMPEACHMENT
T - 25. ADAMANT

A. Face; expression on a face
B. Read; scrutinized
C. Act of giving urgent advice or admonition as to conduct
D. High degree of happiness; singular grace, as of manner
E. Courage; fearlessness
F. Catering to the baser passions of others
G. Hateful or detestable; obnoxious
H. Without dignity or aspirations
I. Discrediting or degrading
J. Having to do with spring
K. Give sworn testimony; to lay aside; remove from office
L. Convenient or satisfactory for the purpose; spacious, roomy
M. Conversation; formal discussion as a dissertation or sermon
N. Equipped with trappings, accessories
O. Wood or thicket of small trees and bushes
P. Paid; made compensation for
Q. Sail near the stern of a 3-masted vessel
R. Dealing with letters and spelling
S. Small; tiny
T. Impenetrably hard
U. Beat of any rhythmical movement
V. Predatory bird having a long, forked tail
W. Partial excuses; serve to make less serious
X. Flat piece of wood on which meat is carved and served
Y. Pleasing appearance

Gulliver's Travels Vocabulary Matching 2

___ 1. RECAPITULATION	A. Cause to forsake allegiance
___ 2. PARITY	B. Flat piece of wood on which meat is carved and served
___ 3. COMELINESS	C. Highest point; culmination
___ 4. FOPPERIES	D. Caution; heedfulness
___ 5. RECLUSE	E. Act of putting between; intervention on behalf of a person
___ 6. BATTALIA	F. Summary or repeating
___ 7. DEBAUCHED	G. A stimulant
___ 8. IMPEACHMENT	H. Closed as to be air tight
___ 9. SCHISMS	I. Set free; defended; avenged
___ 10. HERMETICALLY	J. An army in battle array or on the march
___ 11. MASTIFF	K. Partial excuses; serve to make less serious
___ 12. ODIOUS	L. Not to be violated; treated as if sacred
___ 13. PROVOCATIVE	M. One who lives withdrawn from the world
___ 14. INTERPOSITION	N. Divisions into mutually opposed parties
___ 15. TRENCHER	O. Large dog of ancient breed
___ 16. CONFEDERACY	P. Discrediting or degrading
___ 17. ZENITH	Q. Swelling of lymphatic glands
___ 18. VINDICATED	R. Hateful or detestable; obnoxious
___ 19. ADAMANT	S. Manners, etc. of a foolish person
___ 20. EXTENUATIONS	T. Units of distance, each equal to 3 miles
___ 21. SCROFULOUS	U. Pleasing appearance
___ 22. LEAGUES	V. Impenetrably hard
___ 23. CIRCUMSPECTION	W. League or alliance
___ 24. COMMODIOUS	X. Convenient or satisfactory for the purpose; spacious, roomy
___ 25. INVIOLABLE	Y. Equality

Gulliver's Travels Vocabulary Matching 2 Answer Key

F - 1.	RECAPITULATION	A. Cause to forsake allegiance
Y - 2.	PARITY	B. Flat piece of wood on which meat is carved and served
U - 3.	COMELINESS	C. Highest point; culmination
S - 4.	FOPPERIES	D. Caution; heedfulness
M - 5.	RECLUSE	E. Act of putting between; intervention on behalf of a person
J - 6.	BATTALIA	F. Summary or repeating
A - 7.	DEBAUCHED	G. A stimulant
P - 8.	IMPEACHMENT	H. Closed as to be air tight
N - 9.	SCHISMS	I. Set free; defended; avenged
H - 10.	HERMETICALLY	J. An army in battle array or on the march
O - 11.	MASTIFF	K. Partial excuses; serve to make less serious
R - 12.	ODIOUS	L. Not to be violated; treated as if sacred
G - 13.	PROVOCATIVE	M. One who lives withdrawn from the world
E - 14.	INTERPOSITION	N. Divisions into mutually opposed parties
B - 15.	TRENCHER	O. Large dog of ancient breed
W - 16.	CONFEDERACY	P. Discrediting or degrading
C - 17.	ZENITH	Q. Swelling of lymphatic glands
I - 18.	VINDICATED	R. Hateful or detestable; obnoxious
V - 19.	ADAMANT	S. Manners, etc. of a foolish person
K - 20.	EXTENUATIONS	T. Units of distance, each equal to 3 miles
Q - 21.	SCROFULOUS	U. Pleasing appearance
T - 22.	LEAGUES	V. Impenetrably hard
D - 23.	CIRCUMSPECTION	W. League or alliance
X - 24.	COMMODIOUS	X. Convenient or satisfactory for the purpose; spacious, roomy
L - 25.	INVIOLABLE	Y. Equality

Gulliver's Travels Vocabulary Matching 3

___ 1. SCHISMS	A. Convenient or satisfactory for the purpose; spacious, roomy
___ 2. MASTIFF	B. Manners, etc. of a foolish person
___ 3. SCRUPULOUS	C. Trellis or framework on which trees or shrubs are trained to grow in a flattened form
___ 4. INSIPID	D. Reason earnestly with someone
___ 5. ANIMOSITIES	E. Disapproval
___ 6. VEHEMENCE	F. Characterized by violence of feeling or endeavor; passion
___ 7. DIURNAL	G. Bitter hostilities; hatred
___ 8. ZENITH	H. Pertaining to day
___ 9. SCROFULOUS	I. Dull; without interesting qualities
___ 10. EXPOSTULATE	J. Hateful or detestable; obnoxious
___ 11. COMMODIOUS	K. Deserving shame or disgrace
___ 12. VOGUE	L. Predatory bird having a long, forked tail
___ 13. IGNOMINIOUS	M. Swelling of lymphatic glands
___ 14. CONSUMMATE	N. Divisions into mutually opposed parties
___ 15. INADVERTENCE	O. Banter; good-humored ridicule
___ 16. RAILLERY	P. Summary or repeating
___ 17. KITE	Q. Carefully conforming to the dictates of conscience
___ 18. QUADRANT	R. Natural inclination or tendency
___ 19. PROPENSITY	S. Mistake or oversight; something not intentional
___ 20. DELINEATE	T. Portray in words; describe; sketch or trace in outline
___ 21. FOPPERIES	U. A square; navigation instrument
___ 22. RECAPITULATION	V. Highest point; culmination
___ 23. ESPALIER	W. Fashion at a particular time
___ 24. ODIOUS	X. Large dog of ancient breed
___ 25. DISAPPROBATION	Y. Complete or perfect; of the highest quality

Gulliver's Travels Vocabulary Matching 3 Answer Key

N - 1. SCHISMS		A. Convenient or satisfactory for the purpose; spacious, roomy
X - 2. MASTIFF		B. Manners, etc. of a foolish person
Q - 3. SCRUPULOUS		C. Trellis or framework on which trees or shrubs are trained to grow in a flattened form
I - 4. INSIPID		D. Reason earnestly with someone
G - 5. ANIMOSITIES		E. Disapproval
F - 6. VEHEMENCE		F. Characterized by violence of feeling or endeavor; passion
H - 7. DIURNAL		G. Bitter hostilities; hatred
V - 8. ZENITH		H. Pertaining to day
M - 9. SCROFULOUS		I. Dull; without interesting qualities
D - 10. EXPOSTULATE		J. Hateful or detestable; obnoxious
A - 11. COMMODIOUS		K. Deserving shame or disgrace
W - 12. VOGUE		L. Predatory bird having a long, forked tail
K - 13. IGNOMINIOUS		M. Swelling of lymphatic glands
Y - 14. CONSUMMATE		N. Divisions into mutually opposed parties
S - 15. INADVERTENCE		O. Banter; good-humored ridicule
O - 16. RAILLERY		P. Summary or repeating
L - 17. KITE		Q. Carefully conforming to the dictates of conscience
U - 18. QUADRANT		R. Natural inclination or tendency
R - 19. PROPENSITY		S. Mistake or oversight; something not intentional
T - 20. DELINEATE		T. Portray in words; describe; sketch or trace in outline
B - 21. FOPPERIES		U. A square; navigation instrument
P - 22. RECAPITULATION		V. Highest point; culmination
C - 23. ESPALIER		W. Fashion at a particular time
J - 24. ODIOUS		X. Large dog of ancient breed
E - 25. DISAPPROBATION		Y. Complete or perfect; of the highest quality

Gulliver's Travels Vocabulary Matching 4

___ 1. GROVELLING   A. Dishonor; infamy
___ 2. POSTERITY   B. Learning; scholarship; knowledge
___ 3. RUDIMENTS   C. League or alliance
___ 4. DISCOURSE   D. Bitter hostilities; hatred
___ 5. TRENCHER   E. Caused to forsake allegiance
___ 6. CONFEDERACY   F. Discrediting or degrading
___ 7. DEBAUCHED   G. Conversation; formal discussion as a dissertation or sermon
___ 8. COUNTENANCE   H. Not able to be satisfied
___ 9. ANIMOSITIES   I. Without dignity or aspirations
___10. DELINEATE   J. Sincerity; honesty; purity of character
___11. HOGSHEAD   K. Beginnings; first attempts; elementary
___12. CLEMENCY   L. Flat piece of wood on which meat is carved and served
___13. SORREL   M. Portray in words; describe; sketch or trace in outline
___14. IGNOMINY   N. Divisions into mutually opposed parties
___15. RAILLERY   O. Set free; defended; avenged
___16. IMPEACHMENT   P. An army in battle array or on the march
___17. INSATIABLE   Q. Horse of reddish-brown color
___18. ERUDITION   R. Face; expression on a face
___19. DIURNAL   S. Descendants; succeeding generations
___20. COPSE   T. Banter; good-humored ridicule
___21. FOPPERIES   U. Mercy
___22. VINDICATED   V. Pertaining to day
___23. BATTALIA   W. Wood or thicket of small trees and bushes
___24. SCHISMS   X. Manners, etc. of a foolish person
___25. CANDOUR   Y. Large cask

Gulliver's Travels Vocabulary Matching 4 Answer Key

I - 1. GROVELLING	A.	Dishonor; infamy
S - 2. POSTERITY	B.	Learning; scholarship; knowledge
K - 3. RUDIMENTS	C.	League or alliance
G - 4. DISCOURSE	D.	Bitter hostilities; hatred
L - 5. TRENCHER	E.	Caused to forsake allegiance
C - 6. CONFEDERACY	F.	Discrediting or degrading
E - 7. DEBAUCHED	G.	Conversation; formal discussion as a dissertation or sermon
R - 8. COUNTENANCE	H.	Not able to be satisfied
D - 9. ANIMOSITIES	I.	Without dignity or aspirations
M -10. DELINEATE	J.	Sincerity; honesty; purity of character
Y -11. HOGSHEAD	K.	Beginnings; first attempts; elementary
U -12. CLEMENCY	L.	Flat piece of wood on which meat is carved and served
Q -13. SORREL	M.	Portray in words; describe; sketch or trace in outline
A -14. IGNOMINY	N.	Divisions into mutually opposed parties
T -15. RAILLERY	O.	Set free; defended; avenged
F -16. IMPEACHMENT	P.	An army in battle array or on the march
H -17. INSATIABLE	Q.	Horse of reddish-brown color
B -18. ERUDITION	R.	Face; expression on a face
V -19. DIURNAL	S.	Descendants; succeeding generations
W -20. COPSE	T.	Banter; good-humored ridicule
X -21. FOPPERIES	U.	Mercy
O -22. VINDICATED	V.	Pertaining to day
P -23. BATTALIA	W.	Wood or thicket of small trees and bushes
N -24. SCHISMS	X.	Manners, etc. of a foolish person
J -25. CANDOUR	Y.	Large cask

Gulliver's Travels Vocabulary Magic Squares 1

Match the definition with the vocabulary word. Put your answers in the magic squares below. When your answers are correct, all columns and rows will add to the same number.

A. ESPALIER
B. INVIOLABLE
C. RUDIMENTS
D. DELINEATE
E. CIRCUMSPECTION
F. KITE
G. HOGSHEAD
H. SCRUPULOUS
I. IGNOMINIOUS
J. INSATIABLE
K. PROVOCATIVE
L. EXPOSTULATE
M. ALLUSION
N. HERMETICALLY
O. VOGUE
P. GROVELLING

1. Indirect reference
2. Predatory bird having a long, forked tail
3. Carefully conforming to the dictates of conscience
4. Fashion at a particular time
5. Reason earnestly with someone
6. Beginnings; first attempts; elementary
7. Trellis or framework on which trees or shrubs are trained to grow in a flattened form
8. Not able to be satisfied
9. A stimulant
10. Portray in words; describe; sketch or trace in outline
11. Not to be violated; treated as if sacred
12. Deserving shame or disgrace
13. Closed as to be air tight
14. Caution; heedfulness
15. Large cask
16. Without dignity or aspirations

A=	B=	C=	D=
E=	F=	G=	H=
I=	J=	K=	L=
M=	N=	O=	P=

Gulliver's Travels Vocabulary Magic Squares 1 Answer Key

Match the definition with the vocabulary word. Put your answers in the magic squares below. When your answers are correct, all columns and rows will add to the same number.

A. ESPALIER
B. INVIOLABLE
C. RUDIMENTS
D. DELINEATE
E. CIRCUMSPECTION
F. KITE
G. HOGSHEAD
H. SCRUPULOUS
I. IGNOMINIOUS
J. INSATIABLE
K. PROVOCATIVE
L. EXPOSTULATE
M. ALLUSION
N. HERMETICALLY
O. VOGUE
P. GROVELLING

1. Indirect reference
2. Predatory bird having a long, forked tail
3. Carefully conforming to the dictates of conscience
4. Fashion at a particular time
5. Reason earnestly with someone
6. Beginnings; first attempts; elementary
7. Trellis or framework on which trees or shrubs are trained to grow in a flattened form
8. Not able to be satisfied
9. A stimulant
10. Portray in words; describe; sketch or trace in outline
11. Not to be violated; treated as if sacred
12. Deserving shame or disgrace
13. Closed as to be air tight
14. Caution; heedfulness
15. Large cask
16. Without dignity or aspirations

A=7	B=11	C=6	D=10
E=14	F=2	G=15	H=3
I=12	J=8	K=9	L=5
M=1	N=13	O=4	P=16

Gulliver's Travels Vocabulary Magic Squares 2

Match the definition with the vocabulary word. Put your answers in the magic squares below. When your answers are correct, all columns and rows will add to the same number.

A. REDUNDANT
B. CLEMENCY
C. MIZZEN
D. INTERPOSITION
E. IMPUTED
F. GROVELLING
G. PERUSED
H. VOGUE
I. INADVERTENCE
J. ORTHOGRAPHY
K. FOPPERIES
L. HOGSHEAD
M. ESPALIER
N. APPELLATION
O. NECROMANCY
P. VINDICATED

1. Without dignity or aspirations
2. Mistake or oversight; something not intentional
3. Magic; conjuration
4. Act of putting between; intervention on behalf of a person
5. Trellis or framework on which trees or shrubs are trained to grow in a flattened form
6. Mercy
7. Fashion at a particular time
8. Manners, etc. of a foolish person
9. Sail near the stern of a 3-masted vessel
10. Set free; defended; avenged
11. Dealing with letters and spelling
12. Attributed to
13. Large cask
14. Read; scrutinized
15. Needlessly repetitive
16. Act of naming; act of appealing; a name or title

A=	B=	C=	D=
E=	F=	G=	H=
I=	J=	K=	L=
M=	N=	O=	P=

Gulliver's Travels Vocabulary Magic Squares 2 Answer Key

Match the definition with the vocabulary word. Put your answers in the magic squares below. When your answers are correct, all columns and rows will add to the same number.

A. REDUNDANT
B. CLEMENCY
C. MIZZEN
D. INTERPOSITION
E. IMPUTED
F. GROVELLING
G. PERUSED
H. VOGUE
I. INADVERTENCE
J. ORTHOGRAPHY
K. FOPPERIES
L. HOGSHEAD
M. ESPALIER
N. APPELLATION
O. NECROMANCY
P. VINDICATED

1. Without dignity or aspirations
2. Mistake or oversight; something not intentional
3. Magic; conjuration
4. Act of putting between; intervention on behalf of a person
5. Trellis or framework on which trees or shrubs are trained to grow in a flattened form
6. Mercy
7. Fashion at a particular time
8. Manners, etc. of a foolish person
9. Sail near the stern of a 3-masted vessel
10. Set free; defended; avenged
11. Dealing with letters and spelling
12. Attributed to
13. Large cask
14. Read; scrutinized
15. Needlessly repetitive
16. Act of naming; act of appealing; a name or title

A=15	B=6	C=9	D=4
E=12	F=1	G=14	H=7
I=2	J=11	K=8	L=13
M=5	N=16	O=3	P=10

Gulliver's Travels Vocabulary Magic Squares 3

Match the definition with the vocabulary word. Put your answers in the magic squares below. When your answers are correct, all columns and rows will add to the same number.

A. DECLIVITY
B. IMPUTED
C. NECROMANCY
D. ORTHOGRAPHY
E. RUDIMENTS
F. PRODIGIOUS
G. DELINEATE
H. ADAMANT
I. ESPALIER
J. VINDICATED
K. CANDOUR
L. INTREPIDITY
M. REDUNDANT
N. RECAPITULATION
O. VOGUE
P. SCHISMS

1. Attributed to
2. Portray in words; describe; sketch or trace in outline
3. Sincerity; honesty; purity of character
4. Summary or repeating
5. Needlessly repetitive
6. Courage; fearlessness
7. Impenetrably hard
8. Sloping downward
9. Divisions into mutually opposed parties
10. Trellis or framework on which trees or shrubs are trained to grow in a flattened form
11. Beginnings; first attempts; elementary
12. Dealing with letters and spelling
13. Magic; conjuration
14. Extraordinary size, amount
15. Set free; defended; avenged
16. Fashion at a particular time

A=	B=	C=	D=
E=	F=	G=	H=
I=	J=	K=	L=
M=	N=	O=	P=

83
Copyrighted

Gulliver's Travels Vocabulary Magic Squares 3 Answer Key

Match the definition with the vocabulary word. Put your answers in the magic squares below. When your answers are correct, all columns and rows will add to the same number.

A. DECLIVITY
B. IMPUTED
C. NECROMANCY
D. ORTHOGRAPHY
E. RUDIMENTS
F. PRODIGIOUS
G. DELINEATE
H. ADAMANT
I. ESPALIER
J. VINDICATED
K. CANDOUR
L. INTREPIDITY
M. REDUNDANT
N. RECAPITULATION
O. VOGUE
P. SCHISMS

1. Attributed to
2. Portray in words; describe; sketch or trace in outline
3. Sincerity; honesty; purity of character
4. Summary or repeating
5. Needlessly repetitive
6. Courage; fearlessness
7. Impenetrably hard
8. Sloping downward
9. Divisions into mutually opposed parties
10. Trellis or framework on which trees or shrubs are trained to grow in a flattened form
11. Beginnings; first attempts; elementary
12. Dealing with letters and spelling
13. Magic; conjuration
14. Extraordinary size, amount
15. Set free; defended; avenged
16. Fashion at a particular time

A=8	B=1	C=13	D=12
E=11	F=14	G=2	H=7
I=10	J=15	K=3	L=6
M=5	N=4	O=16	P=9

Gulliver's Travels Vocabulary Magic Squares 4

Match the definition with the vocabulary word. Put your answers in the magic squares below. When your answers are correct, all columns and rows will add to the same number.

A. DIMINUTIVE
B. PERUSED
C. ERUDITION
D. SCROFULOUS
E. COMMODIOUS
F. ALLUSION
G. QUADRANT
H. INADVERTENCE
I. SORREL
J. CONFEDERACY
K. ALACRITY
L. ORTHOGRAPHY
M. ANIMOSITIES
N. CIRCUMLOCUTIONS
O. MAXIM
P. DECLIVITY

1. Learning; scholarship; knowledge
2. League or alliance
3. Indirect reference
4. Axiom; an expression of a general truth
5. Sloping downward
6. Convenient or satisfactory for the purpose; spacious, roomy
7. Horse of reddish-brown color
8. Swelling of lymphatic glands
9. Bitter hostilities; hatred
10. Mistake or oversight; something not intentional
11. Dealing with letters and spelling
12. Small; tiny
13. Read; scrutinized
14. Briskness; cheerful readiness
15. A square; navigation instrument
16. Speaking in a round about way; use of many words when a few would work

A=	B=	C=	D=
E=	F=	G=	H=
I=	J=	K=	L=
M=	N=	O=	P=

85
Copyrighted

Gulliver's Travels Vocabulary Magic Squares 4 Answer Key

Match the definition with the vocabulary word. Put your answers in the magic squares below. When your answers are correct, all columns and rows will add to the same number.

A. DIMINUTIVE
B. PERUSED
C. ERUDITION
D. SCROFULOUS
E. COMMODIOUS
F. ALLUSION
G. QUADRANT
H. INADVERTENCE
I. SORREL
J. CONFEDERACY
K. ALACRITY
L. ORTHOGRAPHY
M. ANIMOSITIES
N. CIRCUMLOCUTIONS
O. MAXIM
P. DECLIVITY

1. Learning; scholarship; knowledge
2. League or alliance
3. Indirect reference
4. Axiom; an expression of a general truth
5. Sloping downward
6. Convenient or satisfactory for the purpose; spacious, roomy
7. Horse of reddish-brown color
8. Swelling of lymphatic glands
9. Bitter hostilities; hatred
10. Mistake or oversight; something not intentional
11. Dealing with letters and spelling
12. Small; tiny
13. Read; scrutinized
14. Briskness; cheerful readiness
15. A square; navigation instrument
16. Speaking in a round about way; use of many words when a few would work

A=12	B=13	C=1	D=8
E=6	F=3	G=15	H=10
I=7	J=2	K=14	L=11
M=9	N=16	O=4	P=5

Gulliver's Travels Vocabulary Word Search 1

```
A P P E L L A T I O N S I M P U T E D M
L U B E C N E D A C U F A Z A M J P P S
A X D M R C A N D O U R D F X S Y P M L
C J P I P U N J L L Y D A W G X T S F Y
R N R Z T G S U B H Y E M F Q H I I C K
I O O Z T O P E P V R L A X F H R N F T
T I P E V U R A D S Y I N L C Q A S D F
Y T E N R N R V X T H N T S V M P I E F
W I N C X G R A I L L E R Y O G S P C R
Y S S D O C X D R K D A L R K G T I L D
N O I H E O I C E E L T C V R R R D I Z
I P T D J P V E H E M E N C E U G O V W
M R Y C E S O C C D N N A D C R T Q I P
O E L R Q E U S N I S Z U G L T N U T S
N T T K O A M Q E S L N D Q U Z A A Y H
G N R P B D H K R D D M R R S E U D L B
I I B E Q B I D T A C A C Z E N S R F D
F M D D X T Y O N I X X B H K I R A D V
S O R R E L J T U N Z I T N H T U N Z Y
H O G S H E A D S S P M P S D H P T P H
```

A square; navigation instrument (8)
Act of naming; act of appealing; a name or title (11)
Act of putting between; intervention on behalf of a person (13)
Attributed to (7)
Axiom; an expression of a general truth (5)
Banter; good-humored ridicule (8)
Beat of any rhythmical movement (7)
Briskness; cheerful readiness (8)
Carefully conforming to the dictates of conscience (10)
Caused to forsake allegiance (9)
Characterized by violence of feeling or endeavor; passion (9)
Courage; fearlessness (11)
Dealing with letters and spelling (11)
Dishonor; infamy (8)
Divisions into mutually opposed parties (7)
Dull; without interesting qualities (7)
Equality (6)
Fashion at a particular time (5)
Feeling, attitude, or show of scornful superiority (7)
Flat piece of wood on which meat is carved and served (8)

Give sworn testimony; to lay aside; remove from office (6)
Hateful or detestable; obnoxious (6)
Having to do with spring (6)
Highest point; culmination (6)
Horse of reddish-brown color (6)
Impenetrably hard (7)
Large cask (8)
Large dog of ancient breed (7)
Magic; conjuration (10)
Natural inclination or tendency (10)
Needlessly repetitive (9)
One authorized to audit accounts (7)
One who lives withdrawn from the world (7)
Portray in words; describe; sketch or trace in outline (9)
Predatory bird having a long, forked tail (4)
Proceeding from and conformable to; in accordance with (8)
Read; scrutinized (7)
Sail near the stern of a 3-masted vessel (6)
Sincerity; honesty; purity of character (7)
Sloping downward (9)
Units of distance, each equal to 3 miles (7)
Wood or thicket of small trees and bushes (5)

Gulliver's Travels Vocabulary Word Search 1 Answer Key

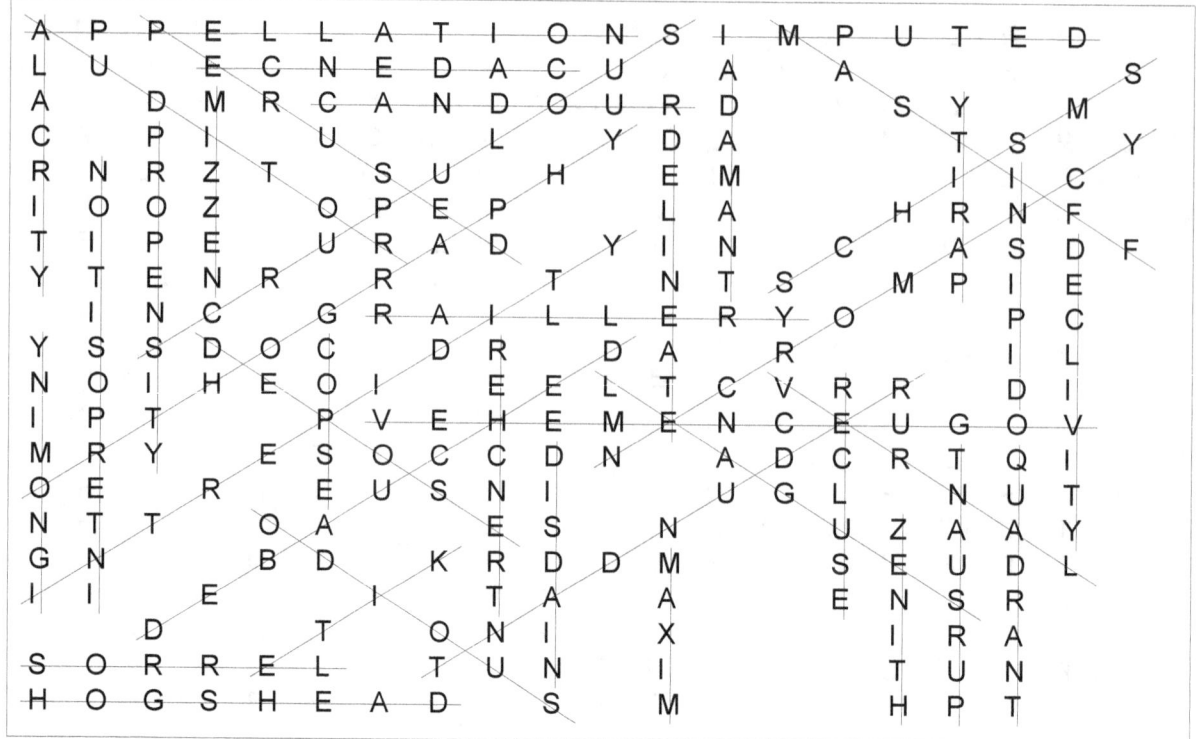

A square; navigation instrument (8)
Act of naming; act of appealing; a name or title (11)
Act of putting between; intervention on behalf of a person (13)
Attributed to (7)
Axiom; an expression of a general truth (5)
Banter; good-humored ridicule (8)
Beat of any rhythmical movement (7)
Briskness; cheerful readiness (8)
Carefully conforming to the dictates of conscience (10)
Caused to forsake allegiance (9)
Characterized by violence of feeling or endeavor; passion (9)
Courage; fearlessness (11)
Dealing with letters and spelling (11)
Dishonor; infamy (8)
Divisions into mutually opposed parties (7)
Dull; without interesting qualities (7)
Equality (6)
Fashion at a particular time (5)
Feeling, attitude, or show of scornful superiority (7)
Flat piece of wood on which meat is carved and served (8)

Give sworn testimony; to lay aside; remove from office (6)
Hateful or detestable; obnoxious (6)
Having to do with spring (6)
Highest point; culmination (6)
Horse of reddish-brown color (6)
Impenetrably hard (7)
Large cask (8)
Large dog of ancient breed (7)
Magic; conjuration (10)
Natural inclination or tendency (10)
Needlessly repetitive (9)
One authorized to audit accounts (7)
One who lives withdrawn from the world (7)
Portray in words; describe; sketch or trace in outline (9)
Predatory bird having a long, forked tail (4)
Proceeding from and conformable to; in accordance with (8)
Read; scrutinized (7)
Sail near the stern of a 3-masted vessel (6)
Sincerity; honesty; purity of character (7)
Sloping downward (9)
Units of distance, each equal to 3 miles (7)
Wood or thicket of small trees and bushes (5)

Gulliver's Travels Vocabulary Word Search 2

```
M I Z Z E N I Y F P C I E V O D I O U S
R E D U N D A N T K N O E D W Y S H C K
D D N D B E J G S V P H M F I R R W T A
P T G I B H T P I I E A C M C F C H U M
D J F U Y C D O Y M P N L M O D I D Z H
R T Z R T U L N E G E I K V A D I C T W
B A R N L A X N J U R M D E P T I I E G
V T I A B B C R G S Z O H T O D N O R M
G N I L L E V O R G D S O R R E L I U Q
R F E W L D V E T E G I N L Z P S M T S
U S Q P Y E C F R O D T S H P O Z P C W
D M C C E L R E H Y I I C D P S N U E L
I A A R U R T Y T K S E U G A E L T J K
M X D S U U U I V I C S C L N I A E N N
E I E G O P V S P T O N A P D R N D O T
N M N C Y I U R E E U C N A E E R T C B
T R C F L K Y L S D R T D R R P E Y O Z
S A E C K Y W J O I S B O I I P V Z P S
C L E M E N C Y T U E F U T S O Z D S C
A D A M A N T Y Z Q S J R Y M F L W E D
```

A building, especially one of large size or imposing appearance (7)
Attributed to (7)
Axiom; an expression of a general truth (5)
Banter; good-humored ridicule (8)
Beat of any rhythmical movement (7)
Beginnings; first attempts; elementary (9)
Bitter hostilities; hatred (11)
Briskness; cheerful readiness (8)
Carefully conforming to the dictates of conscience (10)
Catering to the baser passions of others (9)
Caused to forsake allegiance (9)
Characterized by violence of feeling or endeavor; passion (9)
Convenient or satisfactory for the purpose; spacious, roomy (10)
Conversation; formal discussion as a dissertation or sermon (9)
Dull; without interesting qualities (7)
Equality (6)
Equipped with trappings, accessories (10)
Fashion at a particular time (5)
Feeling, attitude, or show of scornful superiority (7)
Give sworn testimony; to lay aside; remove from office (6)
Hateful or detestable; obnoxious (6)
Having to do with spring (6)
Highest point; culmination (6)
Horse of reddish-brown color (6)
Impenetrably hard (7)
Infer from inconclusive evidence (10)
Large cask (8)
Manners, etc. of a foolish person (9)
Mercy (8)
Needlessly repetitive (9)
Not to be violated; treated as if sacred (10)
One authorized to audit accounts (7)
One who lives withdrawn from the world (7)
Pertaining to day (7)
Predatory bird having a long, forked tail (4)
Read; scrutinized (7)
Sail near the stern of a 3-masted vessel (6)
Sincerity; honesty; purity of character (7)
Sloping downward (9)
Units of distance, each equal to 3 miles (7)
Without dignity or aspirations (10)
Wood or thicket of small trees and bushes (5)

Gulliver's Travels Vocabulary Word Search 2 Answer Key

A building, especially one of large size or imposing appearance (7)
Attributed to (7)
Axiom; an expression of a general truth (5)
Banter; good-humored ridicule (8)
Beat of any rhythmical movement (7)
Beginnings; first attempts; elementary (9)
Bitter hostilities; hatred (11)
Briskness; cheerful readiness (8)
Carefully conforming to the dictates of conscience (10)
Catering to the baser passions of others (9)
Caused to forsake allegiance (9)
Characterized by violence of feeling or endeavor; passion (9)
Convenient or satisfactory for the purpose; spacious, roomy (10)
Conversation; formal discussion as a dissertation or sermon (9)
Dull; without interesting qualities (7)
Equality (6)
Equipped with trappings, accessories (10)
Fashion at a particular time (5)
Feeling, attitude, or show of scornful superiority (7)
Give sworn testimony; to lay aside; remove from office (6)
Hateful or detestable; obnoxious (6)
Having to do with spring (6)
Highest point; culmination (6)
Horse of reddish-brown color (6)
Impenetrably hard (7)
Infer from inconclusive evidence (10)
Large cask (8)
Manners, etc. of a foolish person (9)
Mercy (8)
Needlessly repetitive (9)
Not to be violated; treated as if sacred (10)
One authorized to audit accounts (7)
One who lives withdrawn from the world (7)
Pertaining to day (7)
Predatory bird having a long, forked tail (4)
Read; scrutinized (7)
Sail near the stern of a 3-masted vessel (6)
Sincerity; honesty; purity of character (7)
Sloping downward (9)
Units of distance, each equal to 3 miles (7)
Without dignity or aspirations (10)
Wood or thicket of small trees and bushes (5)

Gulliver's Travels Vocabulary Word Search 3

```
S C R O F U L O U S M S I H C S P D H N
A C C O U T E R E D T I J K T S E T O S
T M R F I J F I E M M S Z N C S I I F Y
T A N U K G R E N C M Z U N T M E P
G S K G P E N Y L L M P R E I J S E Q
S T W G P U R O N I I U E Z D N P I S J
D I V P C E L A M D C P S U F A T R R C
E F O J L A U O U I O I R E L D R E U W
X F S L P S D R U N N E T I E M E D O J
H R I N R L Y E G S F I E Y R Y N N C K
O A G U O Z E Y N Z E R O B R Z C A S C
R Q P C P N C M X C D Y W U O W H P I V
T I N S A T I A B L E H O G S H E A D K
A D C N G Z F S V S R K V M C R E C Q
T P O C A N I D O W A K H H N B T N A K
I M P U T E D P A S C F Z A P A S X N X
O P S E E Z E E S D Y V N L C E U H D C
N C E L L D G E L Y A E O I U R O A O R
I K I T E L N M D I T M D G O D I O U S
A W F F G I A I W N N A T U L D V R X X
D B V Y L X P T U M I E I N A E O E P X
S Z M E I K O I V L D A T T K M R L S
I D M M S F C G D O U J T T F P M N N Q
D O Z N X Z T P Q A N A G N E D O A Z M
C D I U R N A L N P B C P D V R C L Z C
```

ACCOUTERED
ADAMANT
APPELLATION
AUDITOR
BATTALIA
CADENCE
CANDOUR
COMELINESS
COMMODIOUS
CONFEDERACY
COPSE
COUNTENANCE
DELINEATE

DEPOSE
DISCOURSE
DISDAIN
DIURNAL
EDIFICE
ERUDITION
ESPALIER
EXHORTATION
FELICITY
FOPPERIES
HOGSHEAD
IGNOMINIOUS
IMPUTED

INSATIABLE
INSIPID
KITE
LEAGUES
MASTIFF
MAXIM
MIZZEN
ODIOUS
PANDERISM
PERUSED
PROPAGATE
PURSUANT
RAILLERY

RECLUSE
RUDIMENTS
SCHISMS
SCROFULOUS
SCRUPULOUS
SORREL
TRENCHER
VERNAL
VINDICATED
VOGUE
ZENITH

Gulliver's Travels Vocabulary Word Search 3 Answer Key

ACCOUTERED	DEPOSE	INSATIABLE	RECLUSE
ADAMANT	DISCOURSE	INSIPID	RUDIMENTS
APPELLATION	DISDAIN	KITE	SCHISMS
AUDITOR	DIURNAL	LEAGUES	SCROFULOUS
BATTALIA	EDIFICE	MASTIFF	SCRUPULOUS
CADENCE	ERUDITION	MAXIM	SORREL
CANDOUR	ESPALIER	MIZZEN	TRENCHER
COMELINESS	EXHORTATION	ODIOUS	VERNAL
COMMODIOUS	FELICITY	PANDERISM	VINDICATED
CONFEDERACY	FOPPERIES	PERUSED	VOGUE
COPSE	HOGSHEAD	PROPAGATE	ZENITH
COUNTENANCE	IGNOMINIOUS	PURSUANT	
DELINEATE	IMPUTED	RAILLERY	

Gulliver's Travels Vocabulary Word Search 4

```
D E P O S E M A S T I F F Z I M Y S V W
E V V V R F I T L N Z P H E G I T C E T
T N S E B I D N V A T X S N N Z H R S
A O C X H C H I I N C U M I O Z V I N L
C I R P R E O O A M O R N T M E I S A S
I T U J R L M U G I I S I H I N L M L N
D A P C A O S E N R A T L T N K C S Y K
N L U B A R P I N T A N A E Y E E P T X
I L L D U N M A I C E P C B S W D E I C
V E O P I O D A G S E N H P L E R R S B
M P U I N T B O U A E F A Y S E S U N C
D P S G M L O O U D T L R N W G O S E B
E A I G E P I R A R I E E M C L E E P D
R H Z C Y D U C B E C P B M U E V D O S
E A V N O S M T R N M Q L F T N I L R L
T W I M Z O D K E O T B O L P L T L P O
U N M L K R P T C D N R J E W V A F D C
O O C J L R E R I C L D A N C C I H L
C F O P P E R I E S U O I G I D O R P W
C P F M V L R Z H C Q X S U N U V P N Q
A N A D A R Q Y C O N Z D E S B O V S C
C Y R E X Z R N U P X A S I Z R O X E
P N Y T I D I P E R T N I P P S P G F X
I X I P T T Q M R S X P N W I K V U F T
N K N C J Z Y G T E C I F I D E V E T X
```

ACCOUTERED	EDIFICE	LEAGUES	RAILLERY
ALACRITY	ESPALIER	MASTIFF	RECOMPENSED
APPELLATION	FOPPERIES	MAXIM	SCHISMS
AUDITOR	IGNOMINIOUS	MIZZEN	SCROFULOUS
CADENCE	IGNOMINY	ODIOUS	SCRUPULOUS
CANDOUR	IMPUTED	ORTHOGRAPHY	SORREL
COMMODIOUS	INADVERTENCE	PARITY	TRENCHER
COPSE	INIMITABLE	PERUSED	VEHEMENCE
COUNTENANCE	INSATIABLE	PRODIGIOUS	VERNAL
DECLIVITY	INSIPID	PROPAGATE	VINDICATED
DEPOSE	INTREPIDITY	PROPENSITY	VOGUE
DISCOURSE	INVIOLABLE	PROVOCATIVE	ZENITH
DISDAIN	KITE	PURSUANT	

Gulliver's Travels Vocabulary Word Search 4 Answer Key

ACCOUTERED	EDIFICE	LEAGUES	RAILLERY
ALACRITY	ESPALIER	MASTIFF	RECOMPENSED
APPELLATION	FOPPERIES	MAXIM	SCHISMS
AUDITOR	IGNOMINIOUS	MIZZEN	SCROFULOUS
CADENCE	IGNOMINY	ODIOUS	SCRUPULOUS
CANDOUR	IMPUTED	ORTHOGRAPHY	SORREL
COMMODIOUS	INADVERTENCE	PARITY	TRENCHER
COPSE	INIMITABLE	PERUSED	VEHEMENCE
COUNTENANCE	INSATIABLE	PRODIGIOUS	VERNAL
DECLIVITY	INSIPID	PROPAGATE	VINDICATED
DEPOSE	INTREPIDITY	PROPENSITY	VOGUE
DISCOURSE	INVIOLABLE	PROVOCATIVE	ZENITH
DISDAIN	KITE	PURSUANT	

Gulliver's Travels Vocabulary Crossword 1

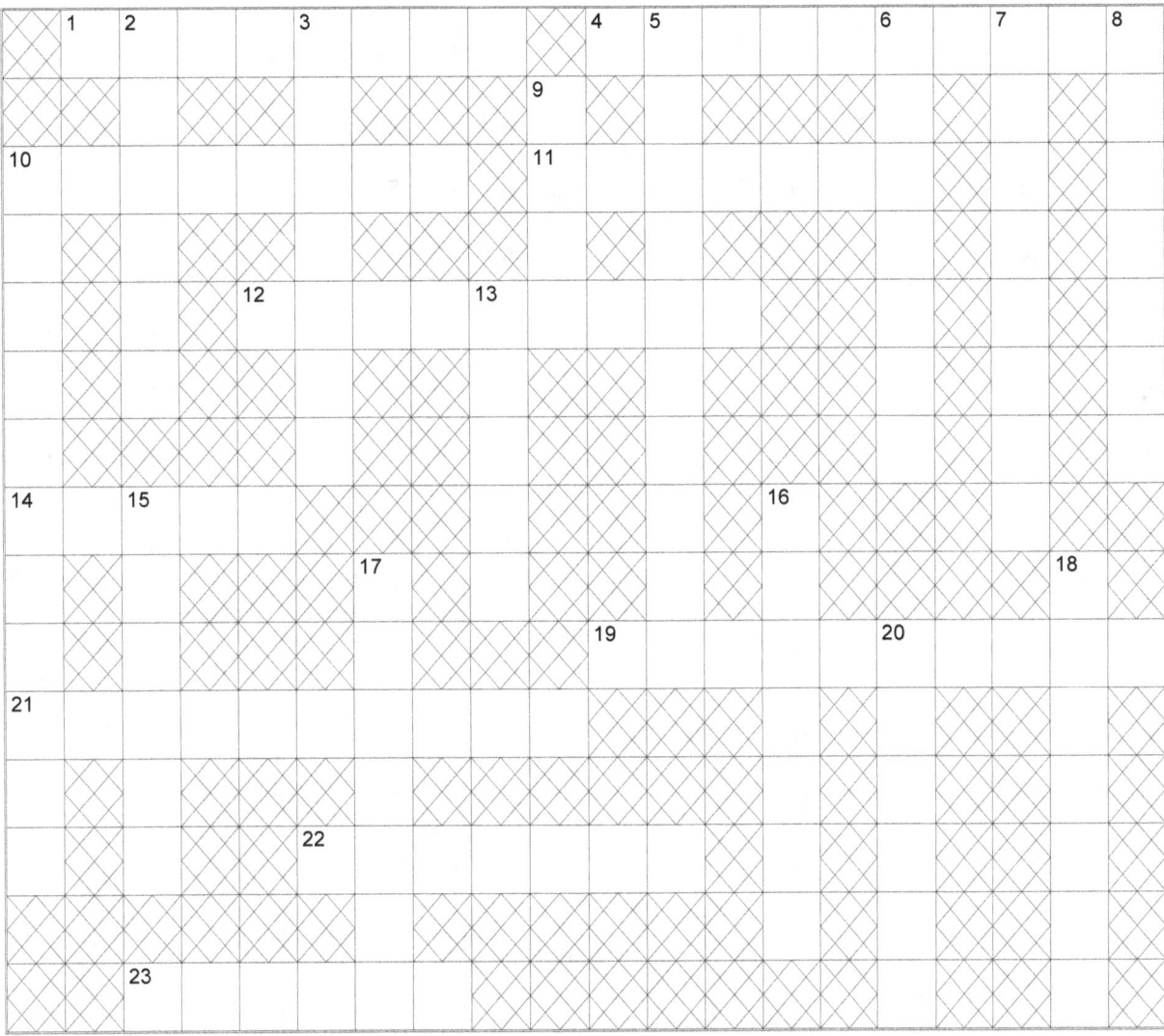

Across
1. Trellis or framework on which trees or shrubs are trained to grow in a flattened form
4. Set free; defended; avenged
10. Proceeding from and conformable to; in accordance with
11. Dull; without interesting qualities
12. Beginnings; first attempts; elementary
14. Wood or thicket of small trees and bushes
19. Magic; conjuration
21. Cannot be imitated or reproduced; matchless
22. Sincerity; honesty; purity of character
23. Highest point; culmination

Down
2. Horse of reddish-brown color
3. Units of distance, each equal to 3 miles
5. Not able to be satisfied
6. Beat of any rhythmical movement
7. Flat piece of wood on which meat is carved and served
8. Pertaining to day
9. Predatory bird having a long, forked tail
10. A stimulant
13. Axiom; an expression of a general truth
15. Equality
16. Read; scrutinized
17. Impenetrably hard
18. Divisions into mutually opposed parties
20. Sail near the stern of a 3-masted vessel

Gulliver's Travels Vocabulary Crossword 1 Answer Key

	1	2		3				4	5			6	7	8
	E	S	P	A	L	I	E	R	V	I	N	D	I	C	A	T	E	D
		O		E				9 K	N			A	R	I
10 P	U	R	S	U	A	N	T	11 I	N	S	I	P	I	D	E	N	U
R		R		G				T		A			E	N	R
O		12 E	R	U	D	13 I	M	E	N	T	S		N	C	N
V		L		E			A			I			C	H	A
O				S			X			A			E	E	L
14 C	O	15 P	S	E		17	I			B		16 P		R	
A		A				A	M			L		E		18 S
T		R				D			19 N	E	C	R	20 O	M	A	N	C	Y
21 I	N	I	M	I	T	A	B	L	E			U		I		H
V		T				M						S		Z		I
E		Y		22 C	A	N	D	O	U	R		E		Z		S
				N								D		E		M
		23 Z	E	N	I	T	H					N				S

Across
1. Trellis or framework on which trees or shrubs are trained to grow in a flattened form
4. Set free; defended; avenged
10. Proceeding from and conformable to; in accordance with
11. Dull; without interesting qualities
12. Beginnings; first attempts; elementary
14. Wood or thicket of small trees and bushes
19. Magic; conjuration
21. Cannot be imitated or reproduced; matchless
22. Sincerity; honesty; purity of character
23. Highest point; culmination

Down
2. Horse of reddish-brown color
3. Units of distance, each equal to 3 miles
5. Not able to be satisfied
6. Beat of any rhythmical movement
7. Flat piece of wood on which meat is carved and served
8. Pertaining to day
9. Predatory bird having a long, forked tail
10. A stimulant
13. Axiom; an expression of a general truth
15. Equality
16. Read; scrutinized
17. Impenetrably hard
18. Divisions into mutually opposed parties
20. Sail near the stern of a 3-masted vessel

Gulliver's Travels Vocabulary Crossword 2

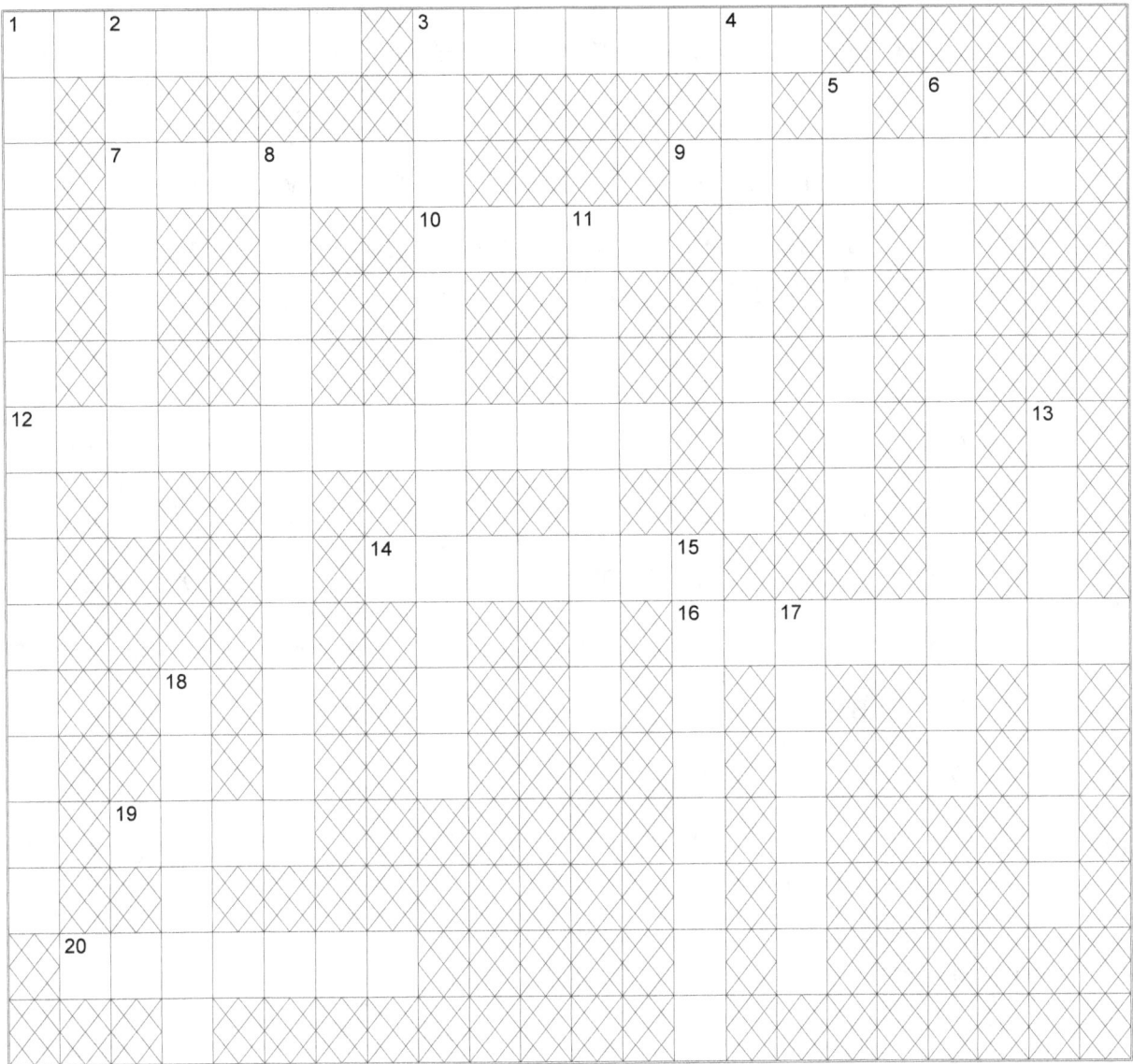

Across
1. Units of distance, each equal to 3 miles
3. Large cask
7. One authorized to audit accounts
9. Mercy
10. Axiom; an expression of a general truth
12. Act of putting between; intervention on behalf of a person
14. Large dog of ancient breed
16. Conducive to a result
19. Predatory bird having a long, forked tail
20. Pertaining to day

Down
1. Unrestrained by law or morality; beyond proper limits
2. Briskness; cheerful readiness
3. Closed as to be air tight
4. Indirect reference
5. Attributed to
6. Courage; fearlessness
8. Unable to be overcome
11. Dishonor; infamy
13. Flat piece of wood on which meat is carved and served
15. High degree of happiness; singular grace, as of manner
17. Equality
18. Hateful or detestable; obnoxious

Gulliver's Travels Vocabulary Crossword 2 Answer Key

¹L	E	²A	G	U	E	S	³H	O	G	S	⁴H	E	A	D
I		L					E				A		⁵I		⁶I
⁷C		A	⁸U	D	I	T	O	R		⁹C	L	E	M	E	N	C	Y
E		C		N			¹⁰M	A	¹¹I	M	U		P		T
N		R		S			E		G		S		U		R
T		I		U			T		N		I		T		E
¹²I	N	T	E	R	P	O	S	I	T	I	O	N		E		¹³T
O		Y		E			C		M		N		D		I		R
U				R		¹⁴M	A	S	T	I	¹⁵F				D		E
¹⁶S				A			L		I		¹⁶E	X	¹⁷P	E	D	I	E	N	T
N		¹⁸O		B			L		Y		L		A				T		C
E		D		L			Y				I		R				Y		H
S		¹⁹K	I	T	E						C		I						E
S		O									I		T						R
		²⁰D	I	U	R	N	A	L			T		Y						
		S									Y								

Across
1. Units of distance, each equal to 3 miles
3. Large cask
7. One authorized to audit accounts
9. Mercy
10. Axiom; an expression of a general truth
12. Act of putting between; intervention on behalf of a person
14. Large dog of ancient breed
16. Conducive to a result
19. Predatory bird having a long, forked tail
20. Pertaining to day

Down
1. Unrestrained by law or morality; beyond proper limits
2. Briskness; cheerful readiness
3. Closed as to be air tight
4. Indirect reference
5. Attributed to
6. Courage; fearlessness
8. Unable to be overcome
11. Dishonor; infamy
13. Flat piece of wood on which meat is carved and served
15. High degree of happiness; singular grace, as of manner
17. Equality
18. Hateful or detestable; obnoxious

Gulliver's Travels Vocabulary Crossword 3

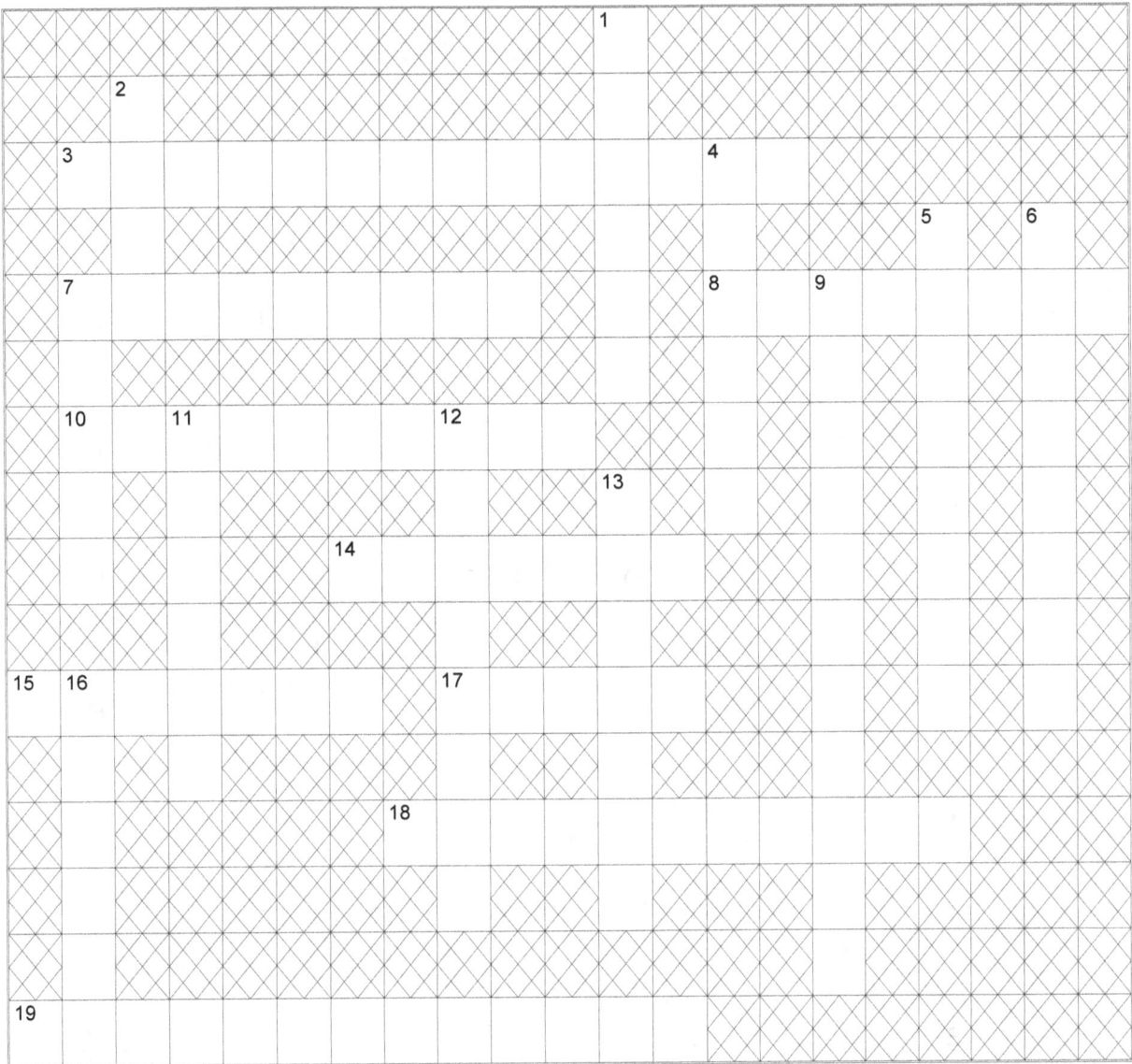

Across

3. Unrestrained by law or morality; beyond proper limits
7. Characterized by violence of feeling or endeavor; passion
8. Banter; good-humored ridicule
10. Without dignity or aspirations
14. Sincerity; honesty; purity of character
15. Attributed to
17. Axiom; an expression of a general truth
18. Bitter hostilities; hatred
19. Act of putting between; intervention on behalf of a person

Down

1. Highest point; culmination
2. Predatory bird having a long, forked tail
4. Horse of reddish-brown color
5. Mercy
6. Flat piece of wood on which meat is carved and served
7. Fashion at a particular time
9. Courage; fearlessness
11. Hateful or detestable; obnoxious
12. Dishonor; infamy
13. One authorized to audit accounts
16. Sail near the stern of a 3-masted vessel

Gulliver's Travels Vocabulary Crossword 3 Answer Key

Across
3. Unrestrained by law or morality; beyond proper limits
7. Characterized by violence of feeling or endeavor; passion
8. Banter; good-humored ridicule
10. Without dignity or aspirations
14. Sincerity; honesty; purity of character
15. Attributed to
17. Axiom; an expression of a general truth
18. Bitter hostilities; hatred
19. Act of putting between; intervention on behalf of a person

Down
1. Highest point; culmination
2. Predatory bird having a long, forked tail
4. Horse of reddish-brown color
5. Mercy
6. Flat piece of wood on which meat is carved and served
7. Fashion at a particular time
9. Courage; fearlessness
11. Hateful or detestable; obnoxious
12. Dishonor; infamy
13. One authorized to audit accounts
16. Sail near the stern of a 3-masted vessel

Gulliver's Travels Vocabulary Crossword 4

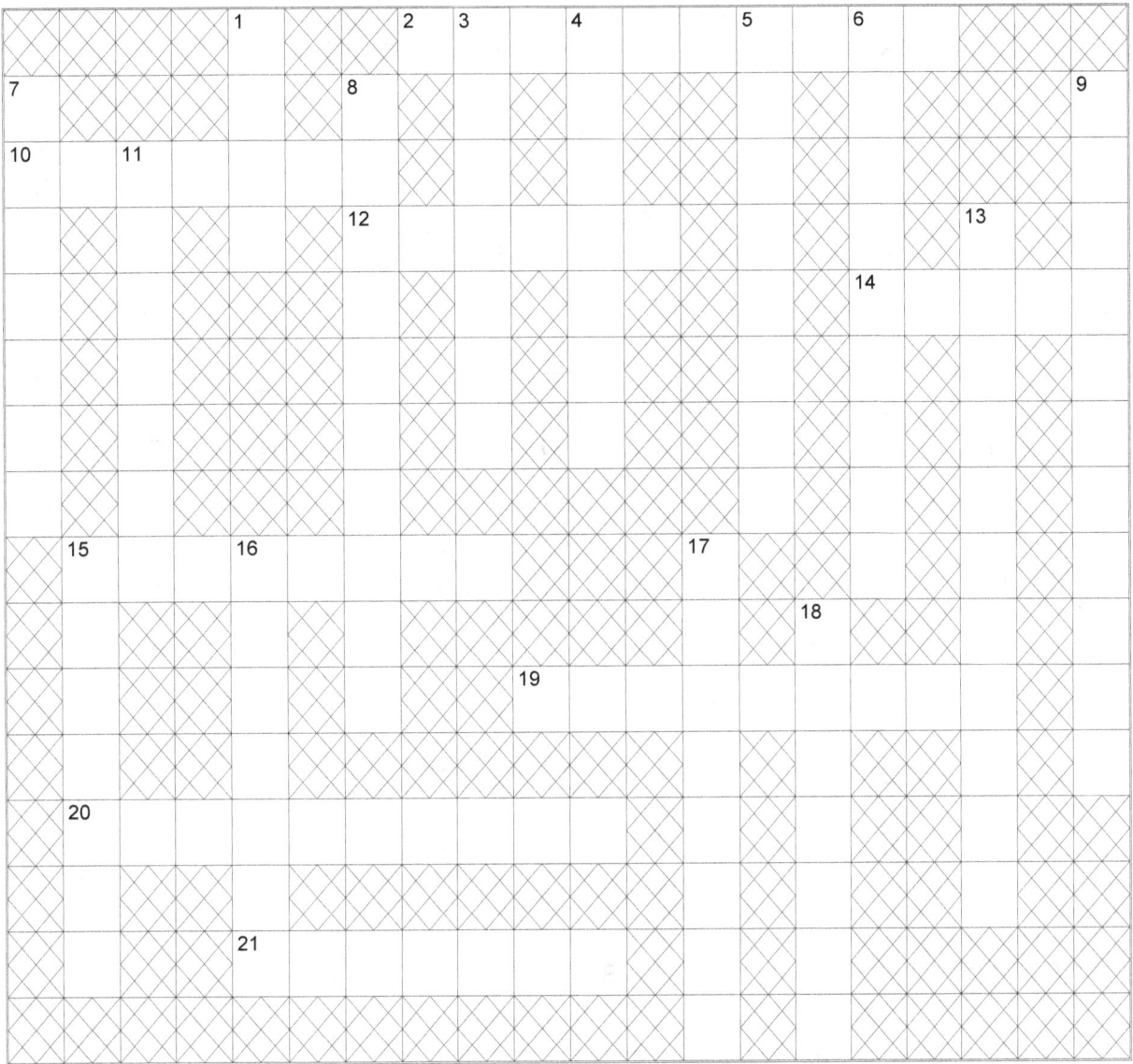

Across
2. Small; tiny
10. One authorized to audit accounts
12. Hateful or detestable; obnoxious
14. Axiom; an expression of a general truth
15. Briskness; cheerful readiness
19. Conducive to a result
20. Equipped with trappings, accessories
21. One who lives withdrawn from the world

Down
1. Predatory bird having a long, forked tail
3. Dull; without interesting qualities
4. Attributed to
5. Flat piece of wood on which meat is carved and served
6. Characterized by violence of feeling or endeavor; passion
7. Beat of any rhythmical movement
8. Without dignity or aspirations
9. Bitter hostilities; hatred
11. Pertaining to day
13. Act of giving urgent advice or admonition as to conduct
15. Impenetrably hard
16. Sincerity; honesty; purity of character
17. Mercy
18. Feeling, attitude, or show of scornful superiority

Gulliver's Travels Vocabulary Crossword 4 Answer Key

Across
2. Small; tiny
10. One authorized to audit accounts
12. Hateful or detestable; obnoxious
14. Axiom; an expression of a general truth
15. Briskness; cheerful readiness
19. Conducive to a result
20. Equipped with trappings, accessories
21. One who lives withdrawn from the world

Down
1. Predatory bird having a long, forked tail
3. Dull; without interesting qualities
4. Attributed to
5. Flat piece of wood on which meat is carved and served
6. Characterized by violence of feeling or endeavor; passion
7. Beat of any rhythmical movement
8. Without dignity or aspirations
9. Bitter hostilities; hatred
11. Pertaining to day
13. Act of giving urgent advice or admonition as to conduct
15. Impenetrably hard
16. Sincerity; honesty; purity of character
17. Mercy
18. Feeling, attitude, or show of scornful superiority

Gulliver's Travels Vocabulary Juggle Letters 1

1. NYCCLEME = 1. _____
   Mercy

2. VIDYLCITE = 2. _____
   Sloping downward

3. SPCROIETCCIMNU = 3. _____
   Caution; heedfulness

4. EMMPCAIHTEN = 4. _____
   Discrediting or degrading

5. XEETPINDE = 5. _____
   Conducive to a result

6. HECEMVENE = 6. _____
   Characterized by violence of feeling or endeavor; passion

7. ORCCEUDTEA = 7. _____
   Equipped with trappings, accessories

8. SFOCSLUURO = 8. _____
   Swelling of lymphatic glands

9. SCUUPULSRO = 9. _____
   Carefully conforming to the dictates of conscience

10. UNOADCR = 10. _____
    Sincerity; honesty; purity of character

11. EURTOAAPICTINL = 11. _____
    Summary or repeating

12. INEIOURDT = 12. _____
    Learning; scholarship; knowledge

13. PNTGIOROSSC = 13. _____
    Forecasting what is to come

14. ROTIOACEVVP = 14. _____
    A stimulant

15. UTAMNMCOES = 15. _____
    Complete or perfect; of the highest quality

Gulliver's Travels Vocabulary Juggle Letters 1 Answer Key

1. NYCCLEME = 1. CLEMENCY
   Mercy

2. VIDYLCITE = 2. DECLIVITY
   Sloping downward

3. SPCROIETCCIMNU = 3. CIRCUMSPECTION
   Caution; heedfulness

4. EMMPCAIHTEN = 4. IMPEACHMENT
   Discrediting or degrading

5. XEETPINDE = 5. EXPEDIENT
   Conducive to a result

6. HECEMVENE = 6. VEHEMENCE
   Characterized by violence of feeling or endeavor; passion

7. ORCCEUDTEA = 7. ACCOUTERED
   Equipped with trappings, accessories

8. SFOCSLUURO = 8. SCROFULOUS
   Swelling of lymphatic glands

9. SCUUPULSRO = 9. SCRUPULOUS
   Carefully conforming to the dictates of conscience

10. UNOADCR = 10. CANDOUR
    Sincerity; honesty; purity of character

11. EURTOAAPICTINL = 11. RECAPITULATION
    Summary or repeating

12. INEIOURDT = 12. ERUDITION
    Learning; scholarship; knowledge

13. PNTGIOROSSC = 13. PROGNOSTICS
    Forecasting what is to come

14. ROTIOACEVVP = 14. PROVOCATIVE
    A stimulant

15. UTAMNMCOES = 15. CONSUMMATE
    Complete or perfect; of the highest quality

Copyrighted

Gulliver's Travels Vocabulary Juggle Letters 2

1. UOECACNNETN = 1. _____
   Face; expression on a face

2. ALRENV = 2. _____
   Having to do with spring

3. MUOOCIOSMD = 3. _____
   Convenient or satisfactory for the purpose; spacious, roomy

4. ROSULUOSFC = 4. _____
   Swelling of lymphatic glands

5. ERIAENTCNDEV = 5. _____
   Mistake or oversight; something not intentional

6. AATPENOPLIL = 6. _____
   Act of naming; act of appealing; a name or title

7. IMTRNESUD = 7. _____
   Beginnings; first attempts; elementary

8. ITOAURD = 8. _____
   One authorized to audit accounts

9. ELAUEGS = 9. _____
   Units of distance, each equal to 3 miles

10. CVNTEAIIDD = 10. _____
    Set free; defended; avenged

11. SITRPOYET = 11. _____
    Descendants; succeeding generations

12. SIUDOO = 12. _____
    Hateful or detestable; obnoxious

13. RDSOSCIUE = 13. _____
    Conversation; formal discussion as a dissertation or sermon

14. ADORUNC = 14. _____
    Sincerity; honesty; purity of character

15. SAHEGOHD = 15. _____
    Large cask

Gulliver's Travels Vocabulary Juggle Letters 2 Answer Key

1. UOECACNNETN = 1. COUNTENANCE
   Face; expression on a face

2. ALRENV = 2. VERNAL
   Having to do with spring

3. MUOOCIOSMD = 3. COMMODIOUS
   Convenient or satisfactory for the purpose; spacious, roomy

4. ROSULUOSFC = 4. SCROFULOUS
   Swelling of lymphatic glands

5. ERIAENTCNDEV = 5. INADVERTENCE
   Mistake or oversight; something not intentional

6. AATPENOPLIL = 6. APPELLATION
   Act of naming; act of appealing; a name or title

7. IMTRNESUD = 7. RUDIMENTS
   Beginnings; first attempts; elementary

8. ITOAURD = 8. AUDITOR
   One authorized to audit accounts

9. ELAUEGS = 9. LEAGUES
   Units of distance, each equal to 3 miles

10. CVNTEAIIDD = 10. VINDICATED
    Set free; defended; avenged

11. SITRPOYET = 11. POSTERITY
    Descendants; succeeding generations

12. SIUDOO = 12. ODIOUS
    Hateful or detestable; obnoxious

13. RDSOSCIUE = 13. DISCOURSE
    Conversation; formal discussion as a dissertation or sermon

14. ADORUNC = 14. CANDOUR
    Sincerity; honesty; purity of character

15. SAHEGOHD = 15. HOGSHEAD
    Large cask

Copyrighted

Gulliver's Travels Vocabulary Juggle Letters 3

1. IFCDEEI = 1. _____
   A building, especially one of large size or imposing appearance

2. LMEHRTALYIEC = 2. _____
   Closed as to be air tight

3. OUDOOMCMSI = 3. _____
   Convenient or satisfactory for the purpose; spacious, roomy

4. SUOMACMENT = 4. _____
   Complete or perfect; of the highest quality

5. ITEK = 5. _____
   Predatory bird having a long, forked tail

6. ELIDCITYV = 6. _____
   Sloping downward

7. NTOIRETPIOSNI = 7. _____
   Act of putting between; intervention on behalf of a person

8. NMOTICCLIURSCOU = 8. _____
   Speaking in a round about way; use of many words when a few would work

9. RAAYITCL = 9. _____
   Briskness; cheerful readiness

10. MBENILTIAI = 10. _____
    Cannot be imitated or reproduced; matchless

11. ITMUEDP = 11. _____
    Attributed to

12. SIIIDPN = 12. _____
    Dull; without interesting qualities

13. TZNEHI = 13. _____
    Highest point; culmination

14. NRALIDU = 14. _____
    Pertaining to day

15. PAENLOTLPIA = 15. _____
    Act of naming; act of appealing; a name or title

Gulliver's Travels Vocabulary Juggle Letters 3 Answer Key

1. IFCDEEI = 1. EDIFICE
   A building, especially one of large size or imposing appearance

2. LMEHRTALYIEC = 2. HERMETICALLY
   Closed as to be air tight

3. OUDOOMCMSI = 3. COMMODIOUS
   Convenient or satisfactory for the purpose; spacious, roomy

4. SUOMACMENT = 4. CONSUMMATE
   Complete or perfect; of the highest quality

5. ITEK = 5. KITE
   Predatory bird having a long, forked tail

6. ELIDCITYV = 6. DECLIVITY
   Sloping downward

7. NTOIRETPIOSNI = 7. INTERPOSITION
   Act of putting between; intervention on behalf of a person

8. NMOTICCLIURSCOU = 8. CIRCUMLOCUTIONS
   Speaking in a round about way; use of many words when a few would work

9. RAAYITCL = 9. ALACRITY
   Briskness; cheerful readiness

10. MBENILTIAI = 10. INIMITABLE
    Cannot be imitated or reproduced; matchless

11. ITMUEDP = 11. IMPUTED
    Attributed to

12. SIIIDPN = 12. INSIPID
    Dull; without interesting qualities

13. TZNEHI = 13. ZENITH
    Highest point; culmination

14. NRALIDU = 14. DIURNAL
    Pertaining to day

15. PAENLOTLPIA = 15. APPELLATION
    Act of naming; act of appealing; a name or title

Copyrighted

Gulliver's Travels Vocabulary Juggle Letters 4

1. FMIASTF = 1. _____
   Large dog of ancient breed

2. AEILRLYR = 2. _____
   Banter; good-humored ridicule

3. IDUSMMOCOO = 3. _____
   Convenient or satisfactory for the purpose; spacious, roomy

4. EODENCSREMP = 4. _____
   Paid; made compensation for

5. XAEEOPTUSLT = 5. _____
   Reason earnestly with someone

6. TUUPNARS = 6. _____
   Proceeding from and conformable to; in accordance with

7. MUITPED = 7. _____
   Attributed to

8. LROPUSUCSU = 8. _____
   Carefully conforming to the dictates of conscience

9. SCMSSIH = 9. _____
   Divisions into mutually opposed parties

10. SGTOCONPIRS = 10. _____
    Forecasting what is to come

11. AYCITARL = 11. _____
    Briskness; cheerful readiness

12. ISNIAOEIMST = 12. _____
    Bitter hostilities; hatred

13. ELEMCSISON = 13. _____
    Pleasing appearance

14. LDIETNEAE = 14. _____
    Portray in words; describe; sketch or trace in outline

15. NDAECCE = 15. _____
    Beat of any rhythmical movement

Gulliver's Travels Vocabulary Juggle Letters 4 Answer Key

1. FMIASTF = 1. MASTIFF
   Large dog of ancient breed

2. AEILRLYR = 2. RAILLERY
   Banter; good-humored ridicule

3. IDUSMMOCOO = 3. COMMODIOUS
   Convenient or satisfactory for the purpose; spacious, roomy

4. EODENCSREMP = 4. RECOMPENSED
   Paid; made compensation for

5. XAEEOPTUSLT = 5. EXPOSTULATE
   Reason earnestly with someone

6. TUUPNARS = 6. PURSUANT
   Proceeding from and conformable to; in accordance with

7. MUITPED = 7. IMPUTED
   Attributed to

8. LROPUSUCSU = 8. SCRUPULOUS
   Carefully conforming to the dictates of conscience

9. SCMSSIH = 9. SCHISMS
   Divisions into mutually opposed parties

10. SGTOCONPIRS = 10. PROGNOSTICS
    Forecasting what is to come

11. AYCITARL = 11. ALACRITY
    Briskness; cheerful readiness

12. ISNIAOEIMST = 12. ANIMOSITIES
    Bitter hostilities; hatred

13. ELEMCSISON = 13. COMELINESS
    Pleasing appearance

14. LDIETNEAE = 14. DELINEATE
    Portray in words; describe; sketch or trace in outline

15. NDAECCE = 15. CADENCE
    Beat of any rhythmical movement

ACCOUTERED	Equipped with trappings, accessories
ADAMANT	Impenetrably hard
ALACRITY	Briskness; cheerful readiness
ALLUSION	Indirect reference
ANIMOSITIES	Bitter hostilities; hatred
APPELLATION	Act of naming; act of appealing; a name or title

AUDITOR	One authorized to audit accounts
BATTALIA	An army in battle array or on the march
CADENCE	Beat of any rhythmical movement
CANDOUR	Sincerity; honesty; purity of character
CIRCUMLOCUTIONS	Speaking in a round about way; use of many words when a few would work
CIRCUMSPECTION	Caution; heedfulness

CLEMENCY	Mercy
COMELINESS	Pleasing appearance
COMMODIOUS	Convenient or satisfactory for the purpose; spacious, roomy
CONFEDERACY	League or alliance
CONJECTURE	Infer from inconclusive evidence
CONSUMMATE	Complete or perfect; of the highest quality

COPSE	Wood or thicket of small trees and bushes
COUNTENANCE	Face; expression on a face
DEBAUCHED	Cause to forsake allegiance
DECLIVITY	Sloping downward
DELINEATE	Portray in words; describe; sketch or trace in outline
DEPOSE	Give sworn testimony; to lay aside; remove from office

DIMINUTIVE	Small; tiny
DISAPPROBATION	Disapproval
DISCOURSE	Conversation; formal discussion as a dissertation or sermon
DISDAIN	Feeling, attitude, or show of scornful superiority
DIURNAL	Pertaining to day
EDIFICE	A building, especially one of large size or imposing appearance

ERUDITION	Learning; scholarship; knowledge
ESPALIER	Trellis or framework on which trees or shrubs are trained to grow in a flattened form
EXHORTATION	Act of giving urgent advice or admonition as to conduct
EXPEDIENT	Conducive to a result
EXPOSTULATE	Reason earnestly with someone
EXTENUATIONS	Partial excuses; serve to make less serious

FELICITY	High degree of happiness; singular grace, as of manner
FOPPERIES	Manners, etc. of a foolish person
GROVELLING	Without dignity or aspirations
HERMETICALLY	Closed as to be air tight
HOGSHEAD	Large cask
IGNOMINIOUS	Deserving shame or disgrace

IGNOMINY	Dishonor; infamy
IMPEACHMENT	Discrediting or degrading
IMPUTED	Attributed to
INADVERTENCE	Mistake or oversight; something not intentional
INIMITABLE	Cannot be imitated or reproduced; matchless
INSATIABLE	Not able to be satisfied

INSIPID	Dull; without interesting qualities
INSUPERABLE	Unable to be overcome
INTERPOSITION	Act of putting between; intervention on behalf of a person
INTREPIDITY	Courage; fearlessness
INVIOLABLE	Not to be violated; treated as if sacred
KITE	Predatory bird having a long, forked tail

LEAGUES	Units of distance, each equal to 3 miles
LICENTIOUSNESS	Unrestrained by law or morality; beyond proper limits
MASTIFF	Large dog of ancient breed
MAXIM	Axiom; an expression of a general truth
MIZZEN	Sail near the stern of a 3-masted vessel
NECROMANCY	Magic; conjuration

ODIOUS	Hateful or detestable; obnoxious
ORTHOGRAPHY	Dealing with letters and spelling
PANDERISM	Catering to the baser passions of others
PARITY	Equality
PERUSED	Read; scrutinized
POSTERITY	Descendants; succeeding generations

PRODIGIOUS	Extraordinary size, amount
PROGNOSTICS	Forecasting what is to come
PROPAGATE	Cause animals to multiply or breed
PROPENSITY	Natural inclination or tendency
PROVOCATIVE	A stimulant
PURSUANT	Proceeding from and conformable to; in accordance with

QUADRANT	A square; navigation instrument
RAILLERY	Banter; good-humored ridicule
RECAPITULATION	Summary or repeating
RECLUSE	One who lives withdrawn from the world
RECOMPENSED	Paid; made compensation for
REDUNDANT	Needlessly repetitive

RUDIMENTS	Beginnings; first attempts; elementary
SCHISMS	Divisions into mutually opposed parties
SCROFULOUS	Swelling of lymphatic glands
SCRUPULOUS	Carefully conforming to the dictates of conscience
SORREL	Horse of reddish-brown color
TRENCHER	Flat piece of wood on which meat is carved and served

VEHEMENCE	Characterized by violence of feeling or endeavor; passion
VERNAL	Having to do with spring
VINDICATED	Set free; defended; avenged
VOGUE	Fashion at a particular time
ZENITH	Highest point; culmination

Gulliver's Travels Vocabulary

ADAMANT	DISAPPROBATION	INADVERTENCE	ERUDITION	RUDIMENTS
INIMITABLE	RAILLERY	DEBAUCHED	ALACRITY	PROGNOSTICS
PANDERISM	PROPAGATE	FREE SPACE	CIRCUMLOCUTIONS	CIRCUMSPECTION
APPELLATION	INSIPID	EXHORTATION	LICENTIOUSNESS	EXPEDIENT
RECOMPENSED	DECLIVITY	DELINEATE	CLEMENCY	FOPPERIES

Gulliver's Travels Vocabulary

DISDAIN	INSATIABLE	PROVOCATIVE	FELICITY	COMMODIOUS
PERUSED	TRENCHER	ORTHOGRAPHY	HERMETICALLY	IMPUTED
VERNAL	IGNOMINIOUS	FREE SPACE	VEHEMENCE	ACCOUTERED
CONFEDERACY	INVIOLABLE	QUADRANT	CONSUMMATE	PROPENSITY
SORREL	CONJECTURE	KITE	VOGUE	RECAPITULATION

Gulliver's Travels Vocabulary

KITE	NECROMANCY	PURSUANT	ALLUSION	MAXIM
EDIFICE	EXPOSTULATE	LEAGUES	ORTHOGRAPHY	DIMINUTIVE
HERMETICALLY	RECLUSE	FREE SPACE	INADVERTENCE	COUNTENANCE
SCROFULOUS	PANDERISM	DISDAIN	PROPENSITY	DELINEATE
PARITY	APPELLATION	INSUPERABLE	VEHEMENCE	ADAMANT

Gulliver's Travels Vocabulary

MIZZEN	CONSUMMATE	VERNAL	LICENTIOUSNESS	PRODIGIOUS
DIURNAL	ALACRITY	RUDIMENTS	IMPUTED	BATTALIA
GROVELLING	PERUSED	FREE SPACE	IGNOMINIOUS	EXHORTATION
PROGNOSTICS	INSIPID	PROVOCATIVE	VINDICATED	AUDITOR
COMELINESS	IGNOMINY	CONJECTURE	SCHISMS	INIMITABLE

Gulliver's Travels Vocabulary

ACCOUTERED	INTERPOSITION	CONSUMMATE	TRENCHER	ZENITH
APPELLATION	PROVOCATIVE	SORREL	MAXIM	GROVELLING
EXTENUATIONS	RUDIMENTS	FREE SPACE	IMPUTED	IMPEACHMENT
INIMITABLE	DEPOSE	RECAPITULATION	VERNAL	RECOMPENSED
EXPEDIENT	INSIPID	IGNOMINY	CIRCUMLOCUTIONS	PARITY

Gulliver's Travels Vocabulary

ANIMOSITIES	FELICITY	VOGUE	ADAMANT	HERMETICALLY
FOPPERIES	COMMODIOUS	VINDICATED	DEBAUCHED	CLEMENCY
ESPALIER	SCHISMS	FREE SPACE	ALACRITY	HOGSHEAD
NECROMANCY	COUNTENANCE	ODIOUS	ERUDITION	SCRUPULOUS
DISAPPROBATION	RAILLERY	INSATIABLE	ALLUSION	BATTALIA

Gulliver's Travels Vocabulary

CADENCE	LICENTIOUSNESS	POSTERITY	CLEMENCY	CONJECTURE
CIRCUMSPECTION	KITE	DISAPPROBATION	ADAMANT	ESPALIER
DIURNAL	COMELINESS	FREE SPACE	COUNTENANCE	FELICITY
PROPAGATE	ALLUSION	ZENITH	RUDIMENTS	VEHEMENCE
BATTALIA	DELINEATE	ODIOUS	EXTENUATIONS	DISDAIN

Gulliver's Travels Vocabulary

ALACRITY	SCHISMS	INVIOLABLE	DISCOURSE	APPELLATION
ANIMOSITIES	MAXIM	COPSE	PROGNOSTICS	RECAPITULATION
EXPOSTULATE	MASTIFF	FREE SPACE	PROVOCATIVE	HERMETICALLY
PURSUANT	SCRUPULOUS	PERUSED	LEAGUES	REDUNDANT
INSATIABLE	HOGSHEAD	DEPOSE	DECLIVITY	PROPENSITY

Gulliver's Travels Vocabulary

PARITY	IGNOMINIOUS	TRENCHER	POSTERITY	INSATIABLE
SCHISMS	ALACRITY	RAILLERY	CONJECTURE	EXHORTATION
VEHEMENCE	REDUNDANT	FREE SPACE	CANDOUR	PROPENSITY
DEPOSE	VERNAL	LEAGUES	VOGUE	APPELLATION
SCROFULOUS	EXTENUATIONS	FELICITY	PRODIGIOUS	PROGNOSTICS

Gulliver's Travels Vocabulary

PERUSED	BATTALIA	SCRUPULOUS	ADAMANT	FOPPERIES
CLEMENCY	CONSUMMATE	MAXIM	ORTHOGRAPHY	LICENTIOUSNESS
ZENITH	COMELINESS	FREE SPACE	AUDITOR	ACCOUTERED
NECROMANCY	PANDERISM	CIRCUMSPECTION	COMMODIOUS	KITE
DIMINUTIVE	MIZZEN	SORREL	ALLUSION	INTERPOSITION

Gulliver's Travels Vocabulary

VINDICATED	DEPOSE	DIMINUTIVE	DISAPPROBATION	ALACRITY
IMPUTED	COUNTENANCE	ERUDITION	IGNOMINY	PERUSED
ALLUSION	VERNAL	FREE SPACE	COMMODIOUS	REDUNDANT
MAXIM	RECOMPENSED	EXHORTATION	GROVELLING	CLEMENCY
DIURNAL	AUDITOR	MIZZEN	LICENTIOUSNESS	RECLUSE

Gulliver's Travels Vocabulary

SCROFULOUS	PARITY	TRENCHER	DECLIVITY	DISCOURSE
CONFEDERACY	CADENCE	KITE	INSATIABLE	INIMITABLE
DELINEATE	RECAPITULATION	FREE SPACE	MASTIFF	HOGSHEAD
ADAMANT	ZENITH	INSIPID	RAILLERY	INTREPIDITY
VEHEMENCE	EXPEDIENT	EDIFICE	SCHISMS	CONJECTURE

Gulliver's Travels Vocabulary

IMPEACHMENT	RUDIMENTS	REDUNDANT	IGNOMINY	DEPOSE
ESPALIER	VERNAL	PROPENSITY	PURSUANT	DISAPPROBATION
DIURNAL	ACCOUTERED	FREE SPACE	MIZZEN	CANDOUR
ADAMANT	VEHEMENCE	RAILLERY	CLEMENCY	DECLIVITY
COMELINESS	SCHISMS	IGNOMINIOUS	EXPOSTULATE	INSUPERABLE

Gulliver's Travels Vocabulary

CIRCUMSPECTION	CADENCE	COMMODIOUS	RECOMPENSED	DIMINUTIVE
KITE	ODIOUS	MASTIFF	PROGNOSTICS	DELINEATE
FOPPERIES	ALLUSION	FREE SPACE	DEBAUCHED	INTERPOSITION
SCRUPULOUS	IMPUTED	PROVOCATIVE	QUADRANT	CONSUMMATE
DISCOURSE	RECAPITULATION	SORREL	EXTENUATIONS	ZENITH

Gulliver's Travels Vocabulary

PROVOCATIVE	DECLIVITY	VINDICATED	HOGSHEAD	QUADRANT
IGNOMINIOUS	EXTENUATIONS	VOGUE	ESPALIER	EDIFICE
TRENCHER	CANDOUR	FREE SPACE	ACCOUTERED	LICENTIOUSNESS
AUDITOR	CONFEDERACY	SORREL	PROGNOSTICS	INSATIABLE
PARITY	APPELLATION	DELINEATE	ALLUSION	CIRCUMLOCUTIONS

Gulliver's Travels Vocabulary

NECROMANCY	FELICITY	VEHEMENCE	RECOMPENSED	POSTERITY
RECLUSE	VERNAL	CADENCE	MASTIFF	REDUNDANT
ADAMANT	DISAPPROBATION	FREE SPACE	CONSUMMATE	INVIOLABLE
INIMITABLE	ODIOUS	ORTHOGRAPHY	DIMINUTIVE	COPSE
DEBAUCHED	PURSUANT	CLEMENCY	KITE	ERUDITION

Gulliver's Travels Vocabulary

CIRCUMLOCUTIONS	DISAPPROBATION	RAILLERY	COUNTENANCE	INSATIABLE
TRENCHER	COMMODIOUS	VOGUE	DELINEATE	EDIFICE
INADVERTENCE	AUDITOR	FREE SPACE	CIRCUMSPECTION	EXPOSTULATE
SCROFULOUS	BATTALIA	FELICITY	ADAMANT	CONSUMMATE
DIURNAL	FOPPERIES	DECLIVITY	CONFEDERACY	HOGSHEAD

Gulliver's Travels Vocabulary

SCRUPULOUS	SORREL	COMELINESS	GROVELLING	INVIOLABLE
REDUNDANT	POSTERITY	INTREPIDITY	DEBAUCHED	MIZZEN
PROVOCATIVE	DISDAIN	FREE SPACE	DIMINUTIVE	PERUSED
SCHISMS	DISCOURSE	MASTIFF	PRODIGIOUS	PROPENSITY
ERUDITION	CLEMENCY	DEPOSE	VEHEMENCE	NECROMANCY

Gulliver's Travels Vocabulary

RECAPITULATION	DISAPPROBATION	CONFEDERACY	PROPAGATE	ACCOUTERED
ADAMANT	VINDICATED	RECLUSE	RUDIMENTS	SCHISMS
MAXIM	IMPEACHMENT	FREE SPACE	DIURNAL	SCRUPULOUS
CLEMENCY	INSIPID	BATTALIA	AUDITOR	CANDOUR
EXPOSTULATE	ALLUSION	IGNOMINIOUS	INVIOLABLE	INSUPERABLE

Gulliver's Travels Vocabulary

CIRCUMSPECTION	INTREPIDITY	PARITY	DEBAUCHED	ANIMOSITIES
COMMODIOUS	EXHORTATION	SORREL	CIRCUMLOCUTIONS	HOGSHEAD
IGNOMINY	DELINEATE	FREE SPACE	DEPOSE	MIZZEN
QUADRANT	PROGNOSTICS	GROVELLING	TRENCHER	DISDAIN
EXPEDIENT	POSTERITY	COUNTENANCE	DIMINUTIVE	VOGUE

Gulliver's Travels Vocabulary

VERNAL	NECROMANCY	SCHISMS	COUNTENANCE	RAILLERY
CONSUMMATE	IGNOMINY	HOGSHEAD	ADAMANT	DISAPPROBATION
INTERPOSITION	EDIFICE	FREE SPACE	IMPUTED	RUDIMENTS
ERUDITION	CANDOUR	ZENITH	DEBAUCHED	KITE
RECOMPENSED	SORREL	INTREPIDITY	HERMETICALLY	DIMINUTIVE

Gulliver's Travels Vocabulary

DECLIVITY	VOGUE	QUADRANT	PROVOCATIVE	EXPOSTULATE
ESPALIER	ACCOUTERED	ORTHOGRAPHY	CIRCUMLOCUTIONS	PANDERISM
COPSE	DIURNAL	FREE SPACE	MIZZEN	CONFEDERACY
BATTALIA	VINDICATED	COMELINESS	APPELLATION	EXTENUATIONS
PARITY	INSUPERABLE	EXHORTATION	PURSUANT	DELINEATE

Gulliver's Travels Vocabulary

PROGNOSTICS	IGNOMINIOUS	PROPENSITY	CIRCUMSPECTION	BATTALIA
INIMITABLE	INSATIABLE	PANDERISM	AUDITOR	APPELLATION
EDIFICE	FELICITY	FREE SPACE	INVIOLABLE	REDUNDANT
ORTHOGRAPHY	COPSE	INTERPOSITION	PROVOCATIVE	DEPOSE
EXPOSTULATE	DELINEATE	RAILLERY	INSIPID	KITE

Gulliver's Travels Vocabulary

IGNOMINY	COMELINESS	MAXIM	VINDICATED	INADVERTENCE
IMPEACHMENT	SCHISMS	COUNTENANCE	SCRUPULOUS	VERNAL
MIZZEN	DISAPPROBATION	FREE SPACE	ACCOUTERED	CONJECTURE
DECLIVITY	INSUPERABLE	ZENITH	DIURNAL	SORREL
SCROFULOUS	RECAPITULATION	ODIOUS	DISDAIN	CONSUMMATE

Gulliver's Travels Vocabulary

PROVOCATIVE	CLEMENCY	APPELLATION	DEPOSE	COPSE
CONJECTURE	IGNOMINIOUS	ADAMANT	HERMETICALLY	RECAPITULATION
RECOMPENSED	PRODIGIOUS	FREE SPACE	INIMITABLE	PERUSED
LICENTIOUSNESS	POSTERITY	INSIPID	CONFEDERACY	AUDITOR
INSATIABLE	SORREL	SCROFULOUS	DISDAIN	DELINEATE

Gulliver's Travels Vocabulary

DIMINUTIVE	EXPOSTULATE	ANIMOSITIES	CIRCUMLOCUTIONS	PROPAGATE
EDIFICE	VERNAL	BATTALIA	ALACRITY	FELICITY
RECLUSE	DISAPPROBATION	FREE SPACE	ORTHOGRAPHY	SCRUPULOUS
DEBAUCHED	RAILLERY	MIZZEN	PROPENSITY	DISCOURSE
PARITY	MASTIFF	EXHORTATION	SCHISMS	INTREPIDITY

Gulliver's Travels Vocabulary

POSTERITY	ADAMANT	HERMETICALLY	INSUPERABLE	MIZZEN
DEBAUCHED	VOGUE	EDIFICE	PANDERISM	COPSE
TRENCHER	LEAGUES	FREE SPACE	SCROFULOUS	COMMODIOUS
SCHISMS	ZENITH	CADENCE	DIMINUTIVE	ODIOUS
RAILLERY	CIRCUMLOCUTIONS	PROPAGATE	IGNOMINIOUS	INSIPID

Gulliver's Travels Vocabulary

IMPEACHMENT	ALLUSION	RECAPITULATION	DISAPPROBATION	PURSUANT
VEHEMENCE	EXTENUATIONS	QUADRANT	IGNOMINY	CONJECTURE
CONFEDERACY	DECLIVITY	FREE SPACE	MAXIM	ORTHOGRAPHY
INADVERTENCE	LICENTIOUSNESS	DISDAIN	FOPPERIES	EXPEDIENT
COUNTENANCE	MASTIFF	IMPUTED	REDUNDANT	CANDOUR

Gulliver's Travels Vocabulary

POSTERITY	ADAMANT	EXPOSTULATE	IMPUTED	CONJECTURE
INTREPIDITY	LEAGUES	ODIOUS	MIZZEN	DELINEATE
SCHISMS	INIMITABLE	FREE SPACE	BATTALIA	COUNTENANCE
PERUSED	INSUPERABLE	DISAPPROBATION	AUDITOR	GROVELLING
CANDOUR	DIURNAL	PROPAGATE	ORTHOGRAPHY	PROPENSITY

Gulliver's Travels Vocabulary

EDIFICE	PARITY	COMELINESS	CIRCUMSPECTION	DISCOURSE
DEPOSE	TRENCHER	ALLUSION	HOGSHEAD	NECROMANCY
ALACRITY	INTERPOSITION	FREE SPACE	QUADRANT	PURSUANT
COPSE	PANDERISM	ESPALIER	CIRCUMLOCUTIONS	RECOMPENSED
ZENITH	FELICITY	LICENTIOUSNESS	SCRUPULOUS	RECAPITULATION

Gulliver's Travels Vocabulary

SCRUPULOUS	BATTALIA	EDIFICE	INSUPERABLE	EXHORTATION
FELICITY	PROGNOSTICS	COMMODIOUS	MIZZEN	RAILLERY
IGNOMINIOUS	EXPOSTULATE	FREE SPACE	IGNOMINY	MASTIFF
VEHEMENCE	INADVERTENCE	VERNAL	APPELLATION	CLEMENCY
KITE	ADAMANT	RECOMPENSED	ODIOUS	PERUSED

Gulliver's Travels Vocabulary

PRODIGIOUS	DIURNAL	CONSUMMATE	CANDOUR	INTREPIDITY
DEPOSE	CADENCE	SCHISMS	ERUDITION	COMELINESS
PURSUANT	COPSE	FREE SPACE	DIMINUTIVE	PROVOCATIVE
CIRCUMSPECTION	ZENITH	DISAPPROBATION	RECLUSE	DECLIVITY
CIRCUMLOCUTIONS	INSATIABLE	TRENCHER	LEAGUES	CONFEDERACY

www.ingramcontent.com/pod-product-compliance
Lightning Source LLC
Chambersburg PA
CBHW081452070526
44586CB00019B/2325